# Freelance Consulting: Provide Services to High Ticket Customers. Build and Grow Your own Gig Empire.

Daniel D. Coffman

Published by Creafe Publishing, 2023.

While every precaution has been taken in the preparation of this book, the publisher assumes no responsibility for errors or omissions, or for damages resulting from the use of the information contained herein.

FREELANCE CONSULTING: PROVIDE SERVICES TO HIGH TICKET CUSTOMERS. BUILD AND GROW YOUR OWN GIG EMPIRE.

**First edition. September 12, 2023.**



ISBN: 979-8215337073

Written by Daniel D. Coffman.

# Also by Daniel D. Coffman

Freelance Consulting: Provide Services to High Ticket Customers. Build and Grow Your own Gig Empire.

# Table of Contents

# Introduction to freelance consulting

Besides buying consulting company, you can also choose to be an independent adviser. That really is the best alternative if you'd like to possess yourself as your boss and when you'd like to have the ability to choose projects you'll function on. Remember that being a freelancer adviser has its own unique pros and cons. By way of instance, you'll want to locate your own customers and also you might possibly not have the capability to get paid steady stream of revenue. Make certain you weigh the benefits and drawbacks until you move and decide whether that remains the trail which you'd love to choose.

Here is how you can become a freelance adviser:

1. Be a specialist. It might be a little difficult to convince folks to work together with you if you're a freelance adviser. But, you're able to get this easier should you position yourself as someone who's extremely knowledgeable about your preferred niche.

2. Build your own personal site. Ensure it is easier for curious folks to get intouch with you by only creating your own personal site. For optimum results, make certain it speaks volume of your expertise and authenticity. It is necessary it's enlightening and content-rich. It has to also incorporate your internet portfolio which contains your accomplishments and tips from industry leaders.

3. Improve yourself a professional degree. Stay along with this match giving yourself a plus or a benefit over the competition. Handiest effort to raise your wisdom and enhance your capabilities. This really is the most useful thing you could to ensure you'll have the ability to give your customers without a the ideal consulting support.

Think you know what about freelancer consulting projects? Reconsider! Below are a few things which you may get interesting.

1. Possessing a freelancer consulting project does not mean pure pleasure. I have read a great deal of articles and other internet tools which gave me the belief that once you sink teeth in to the discipline of consulting, you will have the best

time of your life and also get tens of thousands of dollars without even breaking a sweat. Well, that really isn't necessarily correct.

Being a consultant, I will tell you that really is only one of the very overwhelming and sometimes, frustrating tasks particularly when you're only beginning. You want to locate your own customers (if you're a freelancer), then you're work odd hours specially if your customers are from the different elements of the entire world, and you're going to potentially save money than 8 hours before one's personal computer regular if your customers are demanding.

2. Freelance consulting projects will soon allow one to get direct control of your working hours and you're going to have more time together with your loved ones along other matters which you're extremely enthusiastic about. Employed as a homebased adviser won't provide you additional hours and energy to pay with your loved ones along other matters if you don't simply get a single client monthly. Well, it's possible to choose. You might elect to acquire more time to earn significantly more money or spend additional time together with your family members but get satisfied with couple hundred bucks each month.

3. Freelance consulting projects will soon triple your earnings. That is true when you've already set yourself in your favorite industry of course when people are prepared to invest tens of thousands of dollars simply to receive your thoughts and comments.

## Why start your own personal freelance-consulting exercise

There certainly are a "zillion good reasons," but do not worry, this show does not carry on for ever!)

1. Be treated as a professional.

Generally, your consulting and freelance customers appreciate your expertise a lot more than corporate managers did. There are just two causes of it. To begin with of they all understand are the credentials; nevertheless they will have not seen your flaws and also have not really a hint about your own insecurities. While the saying goes, familiarity breeds contempt.

# FREELANCE CONSULTING: PROVIDE SERVICES TO HIGH TICKET CUSTOMERS. BUILD AND GROW YOUR OWN GIG EMPIRE.

Second, as you're out of sight, you pose no governmental risk. All you prosper makes the man or woman who brought you set to your job appear good, no matter how striking your job, your company liaison does not have any fear that you-unknown into the remaining organization-can maintain her or his spot in the organization pyramid.

You are not gunning to their own job. Your contact person might be alone in the company who knows you. Your entire strengths are perceived as advantages in the place of as risks since your client sees to operate independently and meet tight deadlines without a on site overseer. You have to be fine.

2. "write" your employee manual.

Maybe this should be transferred into the very top of this list. There are many benefits of self-employment (whenever you are work in the home) should you allow them. Some trainers suggest that you decorate as though you should be visiting the very conservative office on earth -detailed with neck ties or high heel pumps. They state that this allows one to attain expert caliber despite the fact that you're seated on your bedroom facing one's pc.

If grooming necessary to generate professional-level work, my career is in pretty poor shape. Loving to groom yourself in sweat suits or shorts also it will not impede my productivity at all.

And that is the purpose of self love employment. You're able to dress, organize your time and effort, play musicand eat bites nevertheless, where and whenever you decide on. All that matters is the task has done needlessly to say, that you simply continue to advertise and which you provide a professional image on your customer.

If you're diligent and selfdisciplined, with flexibility in your scheduling will be heavenly.

3. Enhance your discussions for a fulltime occupation

When you're idle and steadily spending your resources, you can jump in any job deal, however cluttered or under paid. Whenever you have some freelance job in your own plate, then you silent the despair and present your own needs-or also demands? -more assertively.

4. Often your kids as well as other family duties.

That really is a legitimate advantage of freelancing and consulting, but merely to a extent.

# Advisors - suggestions to become an independent consultant

With the continuing international economic catastrophe, this could be the best time for all to receive work that's recession proof. I strongly urge freelance consulting. This is occupation for people that are thought experts or guru on a certain field. By way of instance, in the event that you're very knowledgeable about online marketing, you are able to be an internet marketing consultant. That really is far better in contrast to getting a 9am-5pm job nowadays. Here is why:

1. Work program. Unlike conventional 9am-5pm occupation, you'll have direct control of your working hours in the event that you're a freelance adviser. You're able to perhaps work after work and midnight with just 34 hours a day based on the customers which you're serving. Which usually means that you are able to have additional time and energy to spend together with your loved ones or perform things which you truly love.

2. Salary. You could create tens of thousands of dollars a month for an independent consultant based on the variety of one's clientele. It's crucial that you set yourself as your finest in your preferred niche and which you vigorously promote your own services to increase your register speed. Based upon your own level of skill and credentials, you may bill $25,000 each client.

3. Work out of house. Possessing a lucrative occupation without leaving the conveniences of one's own home could be your fantasy for a great deal of men and women. It's possible to get this to be realized by being a freelance adviser. It is possible to provide your expertise, information, and tips to your customers

utilizing the world wide web or your own cell phone. You may even work on your pajamas if you would like!

# Assessing freelance search engine optimisation consultants and agencies

What is the distinction between freelancer search engine optimisation advisers and bureaus?

The main distinction is obvious, free-lancers act as independent advisers. They truly are usually self-evident as well as their clientele can be localised, but the theory is that freelance seo's will work from anywhere with customers from anywhere.

Search engine optimization agencies provide comparable consultancy services however they will have a massive team. The magnitude of an search engine optimization agency will vary between anything from a number of visitors to countless. Search engine optimization agencies frequently offer you other web advertising services such as website site design, pay-per-click advertisements or display advertisements in addition to search engine optimisation.

Price

Much like additional support established businesses normally freelance seo's are less costly than search engine optimisation agencies. Agencies have high prices including offices and sales teams, fund departments and accounts managers. Most salespeople work independently in your home offices which makes their own paychecks substantially lower.

Most bureaus that an freelance seo's price their job hourly or about each daily speed.

Process

The true search engine optimization procedure which agencies and freelance advisers follow would be usually quite similar. There is a pretty well developed best practice procedure for bettering a site which usually looks something similar to:

Keyword study

Technical optimization

Onsite optimization

Link construction

Reporting

Terminology and also the specifics of every area of this method will differ from agency to agency and adviser to adviser but many will adhere to this formula more often than not. Some salespeople might concentrate on a specific portion of this search engine optimization process like connection construction but many are rounders who is able to finish all pieces of the procedure.

The largest gap together with an bureau is possibly the degree of accounts management participation that could be helpful for bigger campaigns with big manufacturing companies.

Quality

The standard of search engine optimisation work delivered by agencies and accountants varies substantially consequently no real contrast can be attracted along with consequently a business considering dealing using a consultant or even a consultancy it's the obligation to get assurances concerning the reliability, validity and operation of those that you hire to get your search engine optimisation.

Search references from other clients about the expertise of coping together with the bureau or even the freelancer and also assess their customers contributes to google search engine results.

Agency's frequently sell themselves the gain of owning a multi disciplinary team in their disposal composed of departmental pros like connection contractors and copywriters. This may surely be an edge however as usually

# FREELANCE CONSULTING: PROVIDE SERVICES TO HIGH TICKET CUSTOMERS. BUILD AND GROW YOUR OWN GIG EMPIRE.

freelancers may provide a high quality of results and service from having more personal experience in your own job.

Experience

Possessing a staff can give agencies an advantage in this respect but frequently managers are ex-agency employees who've been at the search engine optimization industry longer and so are on very top of their match. When dealing with a company make certain to get assurances concerning the connection with the associates focusing in your own job. Sloppy search engine optimization work conducted under qualified advisers can sometimes damage your web sites search positions significantly more than it can help.

Sector experts

Managing an search engine optimization effort has various challenges in various businesses and usually specialist experience employed in a certain industry may be major benefit. Some freelancer search engine optimization advisers will specialise in a business for example traveling, retail or fund or inside a certain geographic area like local organizations in london. Many search engine optimisation agencies do not specialise in a business because they'd soon come to an end of possible customers (being a service should just utilize 1 site in a given niche to prevent struggle between customers) what this means is that they can become more generalists nevertheless they'll oftentimes have the ability to draw knowledge from various other campaigns at precisely the exact same niche.

Tech

Some bigger search engine optimization bureaus have developed bespoke applications to take care of their customers efforts and create reports. Tech is surely an significant part search engine optimisation but typically the very best search engine optimisation tools are readily available to every one (at a high price). Most bureau tools are all made to create documents and enhance pieces of these search engine optimization process. They could surely help but be mindful there is no spy tool or item of technology that'll deliver you higher search positions - just good solid search engine optimization work is going to do it always calls for the individual signature.

There is absolutely no 1 size fits all response for if a freelancer or service is going to soon be considered a superior fit for the search engine optimization job. Whenever you are searching suggestions I would recommend speaking with either comparing the benefits and pitfalls of each and fundamentally choose depending on the characteristic of these suggested solution and ethics of references.

# Free-lancing for a management consultant

Instead of operating to get a accreditation is employed as an independent adviser or perhaps a freelancer. Free-lancing offers benefits, however it's not appropriate for all of us. As a way to be considered a thriving freelancer management consultant, above all you have to be a self starter.

Advantages and disadvantages of free-lancing

The upside of freelancing as a management adviser incorporate:

· better making possible - there's no salary limit

· greater number of work

· more flexibility to invest some of time focusing on additional pursuits (e.g. An interest or entrepreneurial enterprise)

· the capability to select just those jobs to pursue which are truly intriguing · the capability to achieve a wholesome work-life equilibrium

· potential to encounter varied cultures and organization approaches

· choosing where you want to operate

· choosing when you want to operate

· honing your expertise for a long standing position in an organization

# FREELANCE CONSULTING: PROVIDE SERVICES TO HIGH TICKET CUSTOMERS. BUILD AND GROW YOUR OWN GIG EMPIRE.

· many tax advantages out of functioning by means of a ltd

The drawback of freelancing as a management adviser includes:

· feast-or-famine syndrome - possibly you've so much work that you do not understand what to do roughly small work you stress about how meals will probably property around the desk

· issue in preparation beforehand budget-wise due to yearly cashflow changes

· a shortage of a service system - i.e. No legalservices, templates, etc..

· no possibility of marketing - you're it

· too much versatility over time (i.e. Procrastinators and also perfectionists recall)

· no body to assign to

· no business advantages (e.g. That you will have to cover health insurance, retirement and so on)

Freelancer earning potential

Normal management adviser free-lancers can make between $80,000 and $145,000 (#54,000-#97,593) or a year. The ordinary hourly rate of an selfemployed adviser varies between $35 and $400 (#23-#270) each hour according to which they live along with also the businesses they aim to. At precisely the exact same point, for at the degree of getting, a freelance adviser must first devote time in building their enterprise, media, and advertisements. Setting a thriving freelancer consultancy demands dedication, consistency, and a great deal of self-motivation.

What's the perfect time for you to freelance?

The ideal time to proceed to freelancing as a advisor is for those who have six weeks for a year of living expenses in a checking account, whenever you have made a range of connections by your consulting or industry occupation, also for those who have enough instruction or experience to control a sensible clientele in just a brief time period. With no book fund, you will see much stress and pressure to make superior benefit customers. Without a network, finding original customers will probably soon be more difficult. Without experience or education, signing contracts together with those first customers will probably soon be more difficult. A few freelance management consultants begin their organizations between occupations. It's crucial to not forget to deal with outsourcing as you desire a business enterprise.

The way to start off free-lancing

After making the movement from functioning to get a consultancy or in industry to free-lancing it's vital that you choose the opportunity to produce a home-based small business program. This plan of action will incorporate general market trends, annual objectives, target customers, etc.. Additionally, when free-lancing, make sure you invest in health, disability, and life insurance plan. Contribute regularly into a family savings and retirement accounts. In this manner, you're able to guard yourself in those"famine" times. You are going to wish to select an apt name for the own outsourcing company and place your prices.

# Chapter one: How to provide services to high-ticket customers

## How to pick what core freelance services to supply?

Deciding what heart freelancer services to supply customers could be both daunting and exciting. Whenever you are a worker however which makes tentative plans to prepare your freelancing business, determining precisely the components that you are able to realistically offer is catchy.

You will find so many distinct potential freelancer paths to choose however, perhaps not all of are lucrative, simple to find out appropriate for your skills, or even something you'd like doing. For several services, there is too much rivalry while others, maybe not enough, indicating a deficiency of demand. Then you can find your assumptions and anxieties to overcome that could hide possibly perfect services for the specific expertise and abilities.

What exactly are a few of the variables that you need to look at when deciding what heart freelancer services to supply to your brand new small business?

Let us research them collectively:

Your instruction and expertise

It is a great deal easier to go to a brand new freelancer support field once you have wisdom and experience of this specific field. Your site backup and advertising and marketing stuff will display your confidence and capability in the subject and that is conveyed to seeing prospects.

Consider ways to possibly incorporate past instruction and livelihood experience in to the introduction of a fresh support. By way of instance, a tuned clothier may possibly provide private styling solutions to local busy career women.

Where your organic gift is different

We are all especially proficient at something even when we do not think money may be drawn up from this pure gift. Frequently when young we have been deterred a career course because we did not see lots of classic occupation chances or earning possibility to be needed. Yet with the world wide web, you can find various ways we could adopt our natural talents and turn them in to re market solutions.

Consider what folks keeping stating you are excellent in and invent potential relevant services that you are able to offer. Natural gift isn't every thing in design however it provides you with a very long way when along with hard labour and clever promotion.

Everything you adore doing

Usually what we adore performing is exactly what we're obviously very good at, however that is simply not always the situation. The fire we all need for some thing ensures we comprise the dedication and drive to turn out to be good because certain skill, regardless of pure ability.

If your outsourcing job is something you would like doing if you're a billionaire and failed to need to lift a finger, then you definitely know that you are definitely going to love your enterprise and the lifestyle associated with that.

Now you know exactly that which you enjoy doing. So think about this fire might be incorporated in to an independent support.

Things you can perform immediately

Time is money when you are a freelancer so the faster you are able to work, the additional income you'll get. Quality is critical obviously therefore rate shouldn't overlook doing a fantastic job. But once you are proficient and experienced in a certain field then it's still possible to do the job fast and produce fantastic results.

When picking a provider or set of services to provide customers, consider what you could do fast also. It's all very well being proficient at some thing and using a natural tendency to it but should you discover it reckless plus it will take a very long time, and it is likely to be an up hill task to achieve your desired self explanatory income objectives.

Services in-demand

It is interesting to consider this professional services it's possible to potentially provide. You will find all types of weird and lovely freelancer professions outthere by professional infant name consultants and off ice enjoyment consultants to professional antiques and also expert funeral mourners. Yet it is necessary to make certain there is actually a huge enough market for those services that you would like to offer you.

Providing a support that's also vague, or can readily be accomplished by business people their interns, is going to lead to fewer enquires. Additionally, there is less possibility for increasing your rates later on.

Services with contest nevertheless maybe not an excessive amount of

Despite what you might think, contest is a great thing. It shows there is requirement for an agency and so lots of customers eager to invest decent money for an expert in that specific skill. Whether there are lots of different individuals doing exactly what you would like to complete then it reveals some hardwork and effort, then you may reap the rewards also take high demand.

Nevertheless, a lot of rivalry may potentially make matters overwhelmingly hard. This can be when you have to drill into a more niche service field perhaps associated with a specific industry, special skill set, or even smaller geographic place.

Services with large income possible

Most salespeople need to fit, and preferably exceedthe wages they'd at their previous 9to5 office occupation. But, free-lancers also ought to think about the additional expenses and saving conditions linked with self-employment like retirement funds, medical insurance policy, emergency cash, and also the typical expenses of running their particular business enterprise.

This means you have to earn much more per annum than someone doing exactly the very same form of job in a workplace. Because of this, it is necessary that you concentrate on providing services people will willingly pay decent money for, which can be sought after, and that can be climbed upward.

Services with likeable customers

Yet another factor to think about when selecting what freelancer services to supply will be what sort of client you'll love to work together with. There are various sorts of customers including fellow accountants, services, small organizations, large foreign businesses, private individuals, publishers, and a lot more.

Your personality and manner of functioning can suit communicating styles and styles average among certain client classes. It is necessary you like the kind of people that you would like to bring with your marketing differently you'll start to fear another enquiry.

Services with merchandise possible

Free-lancing and self-employment gives individuals far more freedom than they may otherwise like being a employee. But, outsourcing additionally entails focusing on different individuals' endeavors and being reliant on consumer earnings. With the years many salespeople opt to generate their products to complement or replace customer function and offer an even far more passive revenue flow.

Selling your products through your website is simpler once you've already assembled a standing and presence in a specific area or industry. By attempting to sell services and products associated with some freelancer market, you're able to sell to existing subscribers and clients. This provides an additional impetus to consider prospective services and products that you may desire to generate later on your career when picking upon services to offer today.

Choosing what heart freelancer services to supply customers must not be quite a challenging choice. Consider each the above mentioned aspects, notably what you like doing and exactly what you prosper, and make something—or set of services—which fit your own skill sets and personality.

# An freelancer's manual to providing a world class client encounter

The net is now among those primary mediums whereby modern companies operate, also it has received no lack of major results on the worldwide market. It has enabled innovators and tiny enterprises to compete in worldwide markets they will have been refused use of, helped push overhead and operating expenses, and awarded consumers a near-limitless quantity of choices once they search services and products of all sorts.

At precisely the same time, ubiquitous, international access into the net has also begun to improve the very essence of job, by allowing flexible working structures, hence rendering it easy for practically any firm to keep a manageable presence by means of a world wide, ondemand work force from the markets that matter most for these.

The development of the world wide web and the explosion of technology that is connected also have made it easier than ever before for individuals to hit out by themselves and pursue freelance are their primary or secondary source of revenue. At the usa, the full 36 percent of this work force reports taking good advantage of freelancer chances. This number is predicted to continue to rise, as a growing number of people think participation in some kind of web enterprise. For these, freelancer job ensures choice and flexibility, however in addition, it means a different set of responsibilities and priorities they may possibly have needed as a salaried or hourly employee. Probably one among the most essential of the responsibilities would be to present an superb client experience for his or her customers, that isn't always possible to get a busy freelancer.

Earning the consumer encounter a priority if outsourcing is not something which occurs naturally to a lot of people, nor does this are high in mind, especially for salespeople that are only beginning. Still, it's really a job that's critical for everyone who expects to generate a stable and significant income from freelance job, specifically for people who rely upon recurring donors to the majority of these income (musicians and movie content founders spring into mind).

To assist, here is a guide to supplying a world-class client experience for do-it-all freelancers.

# start at the start

Contrary to popular belief, placing clients first now is simpler than it sounds. The ideal method to get started achieving so would be to earn a skilled and memorable first impression. The very first interaction a freelancer comes a customer will place the tone for that whole relationship, therefore getting this right will probably pay dividends far into the near future. Make certain that you have your site address freelance and handy company cards available all the time so you are going to be prepared to extend a possible new client with each the info that which they will need to get in touch with you.

After a potential (or present) customer will make contact, be certain that you answer in a timely way. Most customers that are utilized to working together with freelancer workers expect a response to some query within one day, however staying in addition to correspondence should ensure it is feasible to cut that down time window somewhat.

Based on the type of freelancer work you are doing, it's generally a fantastic idea to put aside specific times throughout each work day you can devote to reacting to customers, bearing in mind that the hours which those customers maintain. As an instance, business customers may possibly take a reply throughout ordinary business hours, however, the others might prefer answers. Learning the programs and customs of your clients will be able to allow one to reply to most orders straight away, and never needing to disrupt work to achieve that.

# stay optimistic and helpful

For freelancers, the old axiom'even the customer is always right' remains as true now as it had been once the term was coined from the early 1900s. That is because the client experience is tied into customer care, meaning that the easiest way to continue to keep a person happy is to give them exactly what they desire—and also to get it done with a grin. In training, that is not necessarily as simple as it sounds. It could mean being forced to re arrange work to pay for a blunder made by your customer, or revealing understanding if they are in a rush and so are behaving at an less-than-friendly method. Irrespective of what goes on, the way the freelancer claims themselves speaks volumes to clients by what they could get from the relationship within the extended run.

# handle opinions the ideal way

It's also significant for freelancers to understand that the direction that they handle customers while working on a job is vital. In virtually every circumstance, operating on a job to get a customer will demand a lot of give and take, and it's really essential to deal with client feedback nicely. Todo so, it's a fantastic idea to follow a setup procedure comprising the subsequent steps:

- Song attentively—the very first step from the customer feedback procedure is to permit the client to provide you an entire, uninterrupted explanation of exactly what they'd love to improve or change. No matter what problems that they raise, it's really a fantastic idea to allow them to move without interruption.
- Ask questions—when your customer has given their feedback, replicate their petition to them and have anything questions are required to be certain that you're on exactly the exact same page.
- Consider the reach of the task—occasionally, a customer can make a petition which goes beyond the initial extent of this work you have been hired to accomplish. If that's the case, it's a fantastic thought to rent the client realize that straight a way. If the petition is modest, provide to perform it without further fees, with the knowledge that future requests will not be liberated. If the petition is big, come to a agreement on which extra charges could apply.
- Agree on a deadline—talk about the length of time it is likely to simply take to really make the requested changes, and also acknowledge an end date too as a decent inspection period for your customer.

Prove appreciation—in the close of the conversation, make certain to thank the client to their responses, and promise them you are likely to transport out their asked changes properly and punctually.

# insert personal touches

Although larger companies can be able to devote more function for their customer support operations in relation to a freelancer might hope to fit, there is something to be said for your personal touch for a element in the consumer experience. Because of one-person performance, there is a fantastic possibility a freelancer will construct an intimate consciousness of the preferences of each client, and may more easily supply a personalized customer experience. Adding personal touches such as handwritten notes and post-project follow up calls may go a very long way toward creating a loyal company after, and provide customers a feeling that bigger opponents will not take some time or the attempt to make.

# supply payment flexibility

Another facet of providing a world-class client experience for a freelancer is to offer clients with numerous convenient methods to cover your work. Doing this helps to ensure you'll have the ability to give solutions to the broadest range of consumers without needing to jump through hoops to cover you. This is not difficult to perform for salespeople that run an internet business only because they have the capacity to incorporate a payment gateway right in their very own site. If many deliverables are electronic, clients will probably expect to pay online also.

For freelancers that play onsite services, especially for non-business clients, it is a fantastic idea to provide mobile payments via a smartphone or tablet computer employing a system which supports the most recent payment services such as apple pay, because they are so popular by people everywhere. Business clients, on the other hand, are inclined to possess accounting procedures that require conventional statements and check payments. The fantastic thing is that almost all online payment processors offer some facility for issuing bills and monitoring assess payments, and may send automatic reminders to customers when payments are delinquent. The main point is the fact that it does not require much effort for salespeople to become more flexible with the way they take obligations, and removing friction because procedure results in happier customers and a healthy bottom line.

Happy customers are repeat clients

By starting off each client connection on the ideal foot, then keeping it via clear, instantaneous communication, a positive mindset, and a payment procedure which works for everybody involved, it is feasible for freelancers to present a customer experience that is on par with a far bigger company. The very best part is that doing this is not all that hard or time consuming, as long as the crucial jobs are planned off and assessed without exception. Additionally, it is worth noting that keeping clients happy cuts back on the demand for the freelancer to need to solicit extra effort, as their present clientele will always be pleased to provide them longer jobs and urge them. In the conclusion of the afternoon, providing an exceptional customer experience rewards everybody involved, and should form the base of each freelancer's continuing strategy—it is an actual win-win situation.

## Client service licensed—a essential trait for each freelancer

From my viewpoint, particularly when you are a freelancer, client support is not just another method of becoming professional, however, more of the chance to contact your client. And that is essential because linking with your clients is the perfect way to find great comments, recurring tasks and referrals.

Here is an example of awful client support:

This occurred to me two weeks back:

Me: hello ephantus,

Could you be interested in performing a few additional images for our site? We want a few fresh pandas designed.

Thank you!

Regards,

Tiberiu

Freelancer: alright. No issue.

And here is another instance, after requesting a freelancer for a number of providers:

Freelancer: I am awaiting order partner.

First of all, the client isn't your own partner, even in case you've been working with him for weeks or even years. The client is, to put it simply, the client. And you need to honor him, regardless of what.

Second, you should always begin your message using "dear [title ]," or a"hi [title ],","hello [name]" or"hey [title ]". You are searching to produce a feeling, are not you?

How should client support seem like to get a freelancer?

Consistently answer in a timely fashion

While andreea usually works on the proofreading and editing component, I am normally the one which keeps the communication with the consumers. I try to get this done at the initial two-three hours that they messaged us (that is if I am not sleeping).

Here is why:

A) clients always love if these questions are answered quickly.

B) many freelancers take roughly 24 hours to react, therefore, the client will enjoy our solutions better, in contrast to them.

C) when we bidded on work which has not been given yet, replying the client quicker than a different freelancer could win us the occupation, like, through my opinion I might have the ability to convince the customer that I am the ideal option.

Nonetheless, if a customer contacts you seeing a job which you've applied to and has not been given to you however, do your best not to reply the initial 30 to 60 minutes, even since you might appear desperate afterward.

Constantly be friendly and possess a positive mindset

While previously I introduced you how awful customer support looks like, here are a few more positive examples, right in my account

See the way the message began?

"dear craig,

Thanks for your answer!"

This really is a much warmer way to strategy clients then"okay. I will get it done".

The end statement counts also. To begin with, be certain that you put in a call-to-action, such as excited about cooperating with you!. Second, be certain that you finish your message with a few sort words rather than saying anything. Listed below are a couple closing announcements that I utilize: hot respects, kind regards, best wishes, hot wishes, type dreams, best dreams, all of the ideal.

The structure is also significant. Do not write your answer because a long, endless message. Attempt to hit enter after every so often. It will make it a lot easier to read to your client, and your answer will even look far better. Kudos for you!

Always be prepared to assist

Clients may request some additional something out of you, from time to time. In case it does not require you a great deal of time to perform it say ! It'll matter a great deal to them and you will also place yourself in a favorable light.

This applies to revisions. Yes, it is correct, some clients request more alterations than many others. Do not become mad if this occurs. Most of us know that your work is excellent, it can have only been a mistake. Revisions are a standard role in the life span of a freelancer, therefore, rather than getting angry, cope with it and be more confident about it.

Guru tip: simply to be certain customers do not request too many alterations, I let them know that I just offer two for every work we perform. Stating this by the start will stop them from requesting you to re evaluate your job a lot of times.

You could provide a thirdparty, but that is merely to place yourself in a favorable light!

Supply an overall favorable expertise

You cannot imagine the amount of clients praised our client services. It does not matter what you do, so it is essential that the clients are happy at the conclusion of your contract. Obviously, there is that 1% who won't ever be pleased, but that is another story.

- Should you have to re-do all of your work, then take action
- Should you have to do a complete refund to escape adverse opinions then refund all of the money
- In case you don't enjoy your client's mindset and you are cursing the instant that you've entered that contract, then do not demonstrate this to a client. Keep calm and try to find out everything you could do so as to make matters better and your customer.

## Freelancing tips: customers interaction fundamentals

A sizable part of your outsourcing achievement depends upon how good your connection is with your clientele. As a freelancer, you need to have a good platform in place for communicating and interacting with customers. With this, you are going to discover that it's hard to supply a high degree of support to your clientele.

## FREELANCE CONSULTING: PROVIDE SERVICES TO HIGH TICKET CUSTOMERS. BUILD AND GROW YOUR OWN GIG EMPIRE.

Successful communication not just assists the freelancer provide the very best service potential but also reduce odds of alterations and hurried jobs to conquer deadlines. The outcomes of very good communication imply happy customers and much more profitable business for the freelancer.

Listed below are just four of the best ideas for applicants to socialize with customers, in addition to some information pertaining to every :

1. Do not ever presume what the customer wants.

That can be a serious problem, particularly when coping with a new customer. Let us take a good example of a customer who requests a freelance author to write concerning obesity. While one author will proceed and write about the subject, yet another with great communication abilities will melt and ask queries.

In asking such questions, some freelancer must know precisely what the customer needs. This powerful interaction also helps a number of their customers to have a more awareness of what it is that they require. It's a simple fact that not many customers understand or completely understand just what they need from work.

2. Know the kind of customer you're coping with.

All customers aren't similar. Not realising this to get a freelancer can be a possible source of anxiety for the two parties along with also a recipe for inferior labour and inefficiency. Frequent kinds of customers include:

Clients that need too many particulars: this kind may take a lot of the time which you would otherwise be using to achieve the task available. Politely but firmly putting bounds for these customers is a powerful method of interacting together. Enable them to judge the last outcome you create rather than interfering with your job progress.

The clueless customer: this sort of a customer is aware of what they need but haven't any concept of the practice of getting there. They could be challenged. Socialize with these kinds of customers in a simplified variant of the practice of attaining what they need. This may reassure them that you've got sufficient expertise for their desired aim.

3. Do not rely on a single kind of communicating.

Some salespeople are somewhat ill at ease when interacting with customers on the telephone or meeting them face to face. Others don't have any difficulty in communication with their customers through whatever way. For the bashful salespeople, they could over-rely on email interaction. Even though this is fine, some problems are sorted out via a mixture of communication techniques which have face to face, telephone or email.

To prevent future misunderstanding, fantastic interaction between a freelancer and also their customer entails placing significant decisions and arrangements to writing. Great freelancer-client interaction boosts a fantastic working relationship and much more fulfilling jobs.

4. Handle invoices and bills the proper way.

Some salespeople are too considerate and bashful when it comes to speaking about cash. For you to be successful on your freelancing company, you need to go paid. So if you do you freelancer gig a month or two conduct a fulltime writing organization, you will need to learn how to invoice and bill your customers.

To assist you make sure that you are doing this the ideal way, follow the next steps:

- Measure 1: do a bit of research on new customers.
- Measure 2: establish your repayment conditions.
- Measure 3: get to know the customer's method of paying.
- Measure 4: produce the ideal statement.

As soon as you've begun using these hints to interact and communicate with your customers, you are going to notice more happy customers and simpler project stream.

# 6 actionable steps to attracting higher paying freelance customers

Every entrepreneur functioning one-on-one using a paying customer, quickly finds the various joys and disadvantages of conducting your own business enterprise.

As a freelancer, you understand very early how crucial it's to bring precisely the correct kind of customer.

In precisely the same manner we, as freelancers differ with regard to ability, pricing, communication abilities, and degree of professionalism, therefore do the customers we use. For more technical information on selecting the ideal customers for the freelance business.

Not all customers are made equally.

"not many customers are made equally." attract the correct customers for the freelance business.

There are some which can be an absolute pleasure to use, many more who are unnaturally tolerable, and also people dreaded loathsome couple who'll prove to become absolute nightmares however much outstanding service that they get.

However you slice it, studying the way to recognize and bring no more than the perfect customers for the freelancer business early on, could assist skip years of unnecessary tension and frustration.

Attracting the ideal customers is not that hard, but it will require clarity, dedication, and the capacity to stand on your ground whilst projecting an external image that will filter the crap in the stone.

Listed below are just six actionable measures you can take now, to begin bringing higher paying freelance customers for your enterprise.

1. Cost out the deal seekers.

The perfect way for bringing premium quality, top paying customers, is to place your company in a manner that many appeals only on the top end customers that you need to serve.

Frequently, new franchisees will probably place insanely low costs in an endeavor to earn some much needed money.

This sets a dangerous precedent which unlocks the doors for deal seekers, and people that are not able to pay for the authentic worth of your job.

When the design has been put, these customers will forever anticipate the identical amount of support and will probably be resistant to paying when your costs inevitably grow. Before you've got the opportunity to elevate your rates, they will probably refer you (and your reduced prices) to bargain hunters with comparable expectations.

Be cautious about who you use, since you'll never please the deal seekers. That is among the greatest causes of why you need to begin an independent company on the side as you still possess your fulltime job providing you a renewable income. You will not be tried to take inexpensive work which undervalues youpersonally, for the interest of having the cash in the brief term.

Successful business people know the purchase price of excellence and also are pleased to pay you to your experience. Forget about trying to persuade non budget customers to appreciate your job and pay so. Rather, focus on weeding from the reduced ballers and make yourself attractive on the higher paying customers.

2. Articulate your vision.

Getting your services in high need is the ideal that most freelancers strive for during their careers.

Be careful to not ever encounter as desperate or needy. In the very long term, it is the customer that requires you and your abilities.

If you cannot believe in yourself, how in the world will anybody be sure to do so? Sureit requires a continuous stream of consistent customers so as to flourish, however, your focus must be about demonstrating how crucial your abilities and skills are.

Do not play hard to get, however, impress upon your prospects your providers are of such outstanding quality that it might be their loss to not hire one.

A significant part of your occupation as a freelance business proprietor, will be to convey a vision for the way your services are going to improve your customer's business. They are looking for you for as the authority in your area, and also to clearly articulate the way you are likely to bring the advantages of your ceremony to life in their opinion.

Becoming able to impress upon. A customer, what hiring you'll reach to them, creates a better feeling of want and desire. Describe what you could do, the way you are going to take action, and show a number of examples of previous successes, even if at all possible.

If you can create a feeling of this chances in the marketplace, then because their enthusiasm increases, so are their certainty that you're the clear choice to assist them reach their objectives.

Cost gets less of a focal point point if a customer is currently convinced that the advantages it is possible to deliver will dramatically affect their enterprise.

State your costs and do not be scared to request what you are worth. Another way of stating that is"know your value, however show your worth."

A superb portfolio, customer testimonials, and the capability to conduct business professionally (and), will constantly reevaluate hyped up promises and false bravado.

3. Goal only your perfect customers.

After working to a dozen or so various projects, make sure you begin specifying very clearly what represents your perfect customer.

In minimum, take some time to reflect on the usual qualities your very best customers share in common, and also exactly what it was was so pleasurable about working together. Maybe it had been excellent communication, a knack for creative thinking, the feeling of distance and freedom they enabled youpersonally, a clearly defined short, or even a contagious fire about their enterprise?

Do these kinds of customers are inclined to all be clustered in precisely the exact same industry? What additional styles can you identify on your very best customers that permit you to make your very best work?

Possessing a profound insight to the characteristics and dynamics your perfect customer brings to your table, which makes it much simpler to advertise your support to more amazing customers later on. Life is much too short to devote worried, embarrassing, and also desperate to please. Setting up your job to boost more enthusiasm and pleasure is the very best thing to do.

4. Communicate clearly and receive everything in writing.

Before starting any compensated work for your customer, be certain that you comprehend just what results the customer anticipates (wants) in the conclusion of your work collectively.

Ask unanswered questions and let yourself drill down as much as you can, to clean up anything peculiar about your range of work as well as arrangements.

Listed below are a couple of examples of queries you must inquire if the replies are not already clearly specify, during preliminary talks with your clientele.

• what changes would you enjoy our job to bring around for your company?

• how dedicated are you to viewing this project through to conclusion?

• what response could we reach that would totally surpass your own expectations?

• how do we know if our work is a victory, and measurable targets will we be monitoring against?

• what are the major concerns about this job?

**FREELANCE CONSULTING: PROVIDE SERVICES TO HIGH TICKET CUSTOMERS. BUILD AND GROW YOUR OWN GIG EMPIRE.**

Produce written arrangements, comprise progress landmarks, and make sure you say up front just how much any extra effort will cost if necessary.

When there's a chance of alterations and much more work needed once you send your primary job, then make completely clear what the initial terms include and exclude.

Figure out the hourly billing fee for any function that surpasses the initial arrangement. This implies there are no real estate or false expectations concerning pricing directly from the beginning.

If the customer ends up asking changes and alterations, it is possible to refer back to this initial terms and conditions of your arrangement and bill them accordingly.

Clarifying questions are also a convenient method of filtering the deal hunters when they first method you. Request them up front in their finances, and make quite clear exactly what your budget is.

A person with a small budget will be likely going to attempt to squeeze as far as they can from you, as small as possible. This all but ensures unrealistic expectations, which then puts everyone up for collapse.

5. Say no confidence.

If you've got the feeling you're addressing a minimal baller or deal hunter through your first discussions, do not be scared to turn their small business.

It is not worth your time to battle hard to your prices, whenever there are better-paying customers on the market just waiting to be found.

Do not be unkind or insulting, however, you desire to publicly discourage the deal seekers using phrases such as:

• a more affordable alternative could be more appropriate to your requirements.

• if my solutions are not the finest way for you right now, then we are likely not a fantastic match for the time being.

• I will not be a fantastic match for this job at the moment, below the present guidelines.

Sometimes, standing the earth and becoming clear about the way a pricing reflects your worth may earn a client reevaluate their position.

Obviously, most of us want the cash we spend to offer value, but as entrepreneurswe rely on our worth to deliver us the cash we're worthy of getting. Trust your instincts and become familiar with saying no and meaning it.

6. Conquer yourself-doubt.

Among the main barriers freelancers have bringing higher paying customers, is a mindset of uncertainty and distress.

Most people have limited expertise in requesting cash and obviously stating their fiscal expectations.

Freelancers which are fresh to being in company for themselves frequently feel as they are faking it, or like their skills do not compare to all the other experts on the market, which may make it much harder to feel great about establishing an proper fee.

While it's true that a newcomer has less expertise than a recognized business leader, you still understand a lot more about your subject than a customer who is considering hiring one. Somebody on the newer side, frequently has a much better chance at bringing a new perspective into the function, and becoming more inclined to innovate beyond lots of the preconceived ideas pros carry around together.

Never simply accept anything fee is offered to get work, particularly if you're in doubt about whether it really worth the job you are going to be placing in.

When in doubt, anxiety and distress are running the series, which will not lead to creating your very best choices.

# FREELANCE CONSULTING: PROVIDE SERVICES TO HIGH TICKET CUSTOMERS. BUILD AND GROW YOUR OWN GIG EMPIRE.

It helps to understand that feelings of self-evident are normal once you're just beginning. They shift with time and expertise.

One way to quickly track a mindset shift from self uncertainty, is by simply tapping into a range of tools that will help accelerate your business experience. Look to podcasts, books, conferences, media events, online tools, social networking, coaches, and mentors to step up your game.

Selecting to have a wealth mindset makes it possible to determine opportunities everywhere, just waiting to be maintained.

The inner change that shifting your mindset brings, is the complete certainty that obstacles to achievement are random and also impermanent. Caring for your ideas and activities, to intentionally direct them thinking positively about yourself is an internal event which needs little to do with outside conditions.

Get paid to operate less.

It is tough to beat the sensation of being paid to operate less. In reality, each freelancer I understand will be comfortable using pulling in six figures with no strain of a fulltime day occupation.

The best way to make it happen, is to connect entirely with customers who are confident about their outstanding value you supply, and are consequently fully inclined to make certain their payment reflects their thankful conviction.

It pays to work smarter, instead of tougher. The challenge is going to be learning about that which you work with and finding a lot of these perfect customers to associate with.

For those who have much less of a need want to gratify, and fewer customers to concentrate to, a larger liberty to actually dive deep to the job you do require on, opens. Becoming in a position to devote this degree of power and attention to your endeavors, allows all you produce, to be your very best work. When passion and love are poured to your job, the rewards flow outward in each direction.

# Chapter two: Freelancer and clients

## 3 ideas to maintain your freelance customers

This is the reason why devoting sufficient time to keeping clients is essential. Professionalism, private brand, entrepreneur strategy—that features affect the procedure for supplying high-level services. Contemporary freelancer is an independent business operator, not a contractor that is random.

1. Proper expectations in the start

Talk about the project's needs, discuss your procedure and strategy, discuss the method by which the customer is included in the undertaking.

It's essential to be about the same page in the very first measure of this undertaking. The customer has own opinion on the procedure for collaboration and the end result of this. Discuss more than everything.

In terms of example, talk about the ways of communicating. How frequently would your freelancer customer want to have updates on the job and in what manner? Can it be an email, or you'll be communicating every day at 5 pm via zoom or skype?

This can save you from bothering messages in the customer throughout your workout day. Incidentally, one honest idea—when the customer asks for updates about the condition of the job—you're overlooking something. Do not make them request, put date and time eyeglasses of updates/reports.

And exactly the same about what's going to be delivered the notion, the arrangement, the way the customer will get it done, would there be some alterations, etc.. Supplying something when freelancer client anticipated another is a neglect. However high quality you've provided.

2. Talks significantly less, do more

When you're building appropriate expectations prevent telling about solutions that you don't confident you might provide. But try to overdeliver.

It's a massive thing on keeping a client. Promising significantly less, doing more.

Writing a post—include relevant images, there are a few nice and completely free photo stocks. Developing an internet design—launch it, create it dwell someways, there are a few services today for individuals without coding abilities. Launchpad is a fantastic instance of this.

Imagine a customer who must search for images to add in an report. Maybe he was hoping to purchase themspending money and effort. After the customer gets a post out of you with images, it's prepared for publishing. Fantastic experience.

Or a customer who hopes to find jpg displays and receives a true website or clickable mock-up, that's readily available for sharing with coworkers. This matters give another value to your job.

3. Possessing a contract

The next thing about keeping your freelance customers is a contract. Possessing a contract for every single undertaking. Yes, even when you're likely to utilize an older friend or a colleague. Include everything that you're likely to provide, define when and how you'll send it. Ensure your customer knows that he/she will become just things which have been stated in your contract.

Additionally, add in a contract the points which could insure you. For example, write that customer must supply you an answer to your questions about the job in one day. If it would not occur, shipping date of this job becomes postponed for the amount of times the customer does not respond you.

Cases like the you'll find out in your personal experience. But not wait to add them into a contract.

When you don't have any contract, just the customer determines when your support is sent and should cover. Perhaps not the best situation.

At precisely the same time, even when you send everything in line with this contract and customer needs more—it's a chance to close an additional deal, make a new contract rather than supplying services at no cost.

# 11 strategies for freelance clients come to you

Among the hardest things about freelancing is getting customers. Whether you are just starting an independent company, or trying to cultivate your current customer base,.

A few days, the lifetime of a freelancer may feel just like you're spending additional hours client-hunting than really working. Time is money, and you owe it to yourself to use it sensibly.

But you do not need to resort spending money on marketing campaigns or becoming too"sales-y" (that could come off as distressed). There are other, simpler ways to acquire customers—and rather than you're looking for these, they will visit you. Below are my best 11 tips.

1. Word of mouth

This is most likely the best way to land customers without doing some work to receive them. Whenever someone urges you to someone they know, it implies far more than just a polished resume.

People trust private recommendations over just a portfolio, killer resume/ linkedin profile, or even website. All of it comes down to this age-old expression:"it is not everything you really know, but that."

Thus, do great work, and receive known to other people. Individuals who have their own company likely know others that do, also. And those links only may require a brand new site, movie editing, brand new emblem, etc..

Also—do not disregard household and friends. Starting out by performing work for a relative isn't anything to be embarrassed of. Cash is money. Expertise is experience. And you want both.

Key takeaway: it is not the thing you know, but that. When you do great work for many others, you are jump to get advocated.

2. Have a transparent, up-to-date portfolio—and promote it

A fantastic portfolio is nearly non-negotiable. But, it's necessary to be aware that using a website will not ensure people will visit it. To entice prospective freelance customers, you want to promote it.

The other way is to site (which we will reach next).

And do not neglect if they get there!

—have labour samples or case studies

—access testimonials from preceding customers

—make sure that your contact information is simple to find

Key takeaway: do not just create a great portfolio to showcase your own job; encourage that, too.

3. Website (or more just—create articles)

Add a site for your portfolio or online resume. However, before you dive into head-first to the world of blogging, then it is important that you learn your market.

Writing about subjects relevant to this area that you need to operate in provides you an opportunity to show your experience. There's an art to this.

Here's a fast example: you're a wordpress net designer/developer. You might think it is reasonable compose wordpress"how-to" posts. These posts are super useful...but just to people wanting to find out wordpress themselves, but not those considering paying you to construct a website for them!

Rather, write posts which will appeal to that the people that you would like to operate for and become more inclined to lead to a purchase. For example, post a post about how creating a web site responsive may create x boost in earnings. That will grab the ideal people's attention, and are far more inclined to secure you a new gig.

Key takeaway: blogging is just another means to market your own solutions. However, be certain that you write about subjects that will appeal to your intended client.

4. Compose (or make content) to get *others *

When you produce content to many others, you place yourself in front of eyeballs (like those of possible customers!).

The most frequent type of this is guest composing. But, generating content for some other sites/publications does not need to be composing. It may be:

—illustrations

—infographics

—videos (together with your name at the credits)

—pictures (taking photos for a specific post/guide, using a url to your website below)

While generally, the more individuals you're in the front of, the greater, it is also that you are getting facing. Quality is much more important than volume. Here, quality usually means an audience comprised of individuals who may use your experience.

Key takeaway: growing content for other people puts you in front of people, meaning greater prospective customers.

5. Maintain your linkedin up-to-date

Recruiters and other kinds of hiring supervisors research on linkedin to employ. (they have an whole instrument for this specific purpose)

Additionally, linkedin profiles are inclined to show up in search results when individuals google your title (which virtually every recruiter/employer will).

Possessing an obsolete, dusty linkedin will not force you to stick out among the remainder. Be sure to:

—contain a list that addresses your important and relevant abilities and accomplishments

—maintain your expertise and abilities upgraded

—insert relevant job of yours at the linkedin"work samples" region.

—enjoy a crisp searching profile photograph.

—proceed and beyond adding recommendations from previous employers/people you've worked with.

Key takeaway: recruiters and many others making hiring decisions seem at linkedin. Create a memorable first impression by maintaining yours polished and updated.

6. Maintain other, industry-relevant social networking accounts up so far

Nowadays, you can find social websites websites catering to a number of certain businesses, particularly freelance-oriented areas. Based upon your experience, there probably is a stage for you.

To name a couple:

—for programmers—github

—for designers—dribbble and behance

—for photographers—flickr along with photo critique

—for videographers—vimeo

Like linkedin, keep an upgraded profile with related work examples.

Key takeaway: hang out to the social networks in which prospective employers are searching for talent. Besides, you can network with coworkers to obtain insights and links.

7. Network in-person

## FREELANCE CONSULTING: PROVIDE SERVICES TO HIGH TICKET CUSTOMERS. BUILD AND GROW YOUR OWN GIG EMPIRE.

Attend conventions and neighborhood meetups. Proceed to happy hours. And be certain that you bring some cards!

Meeting face is obviously more memorable—there is that in-person relationship you cannot find online.

Attend events and conventions that are related to your interests. Or, perhaps more importantly, ones which are connected to the interests of the prospective customers (e.g. If you are a graphic designer, then visiting local small business proprietor meetups).

Key takeaway: actually with our technological progress, nothing contrasts to facial websites.

8. Start co-working

Coworking is similar to another kind of in-house media. The most important distinction is that you generally visit some coworking area over the daily, or semi-regularly.

Coworking spaces are all buildings or massive rooms utilized by teams of entrepreneurs/small company owners/freelancers. They are perfect for getting employment (especially freelancer job) at a collaborative environment

In addition, that a coworking area is a fantastic spot to create buddies, as being a freelancer could get lonely. (it is similar to your normal office life, in which you're surrounded by colleagues without the substitute for your own.) Network with other people, collaborate, and also receive your work done.

Key takeaway: coworking has many added benefits, such as networking with other people who may want your solutions.

9. Discuss at events/conferences

1 step from attending events is talking at them. The best types of events/ conferences to talk at are those in which audience members might require your services.

For example, you're a internet designer. Today, every company needs to have a site (made simple by firms such as brandcast—that provide a killer end-to-end internet design platform for specialist designers) so talking at a seminar for company owners are going to become many possible customers to recall your own name. And should you give a discussion about the significance of good site design in company, outlining all advantages it may bring (more period on site, greater visitor participation, more earnings, etc.), then you are going to demonstrate your worth even further.

Needless to say, when it comes to landing talking gigs, you must begin small. However, as you develop credibility because of an remarkable speaker, it is possible to get paid to talk sometimes. Boost your new, get new customers, and get compensated for this? Sounds too good to be true.

Key takeaway: discussing engagements fortify you as an authority in your area. They also give the chance to get before new prospective customers.

10. Network online

Now you do not need to be face-to-face to community. Now you can attend seminars virtually.

For example:

—for programmers—hack.summit

—for online business people—1 day business breakthrough

—for internet creative small business owners—maker mentors

Over online conventions or events, you will find industry-specific forums it is possible to partake in.

—quora—a bunch of different questions you can reply, revealing your understanding on the subject

—freelancers union hives—needs a membership using freelancers union, but is an excellent place to talk about the intricacies of administering

## FREELANCE CONSULTING: PROVIDE SERVICES TO HIGH TICKET CUSTOMERS. BUILD AND GROW YOUR OWN GIG EMPIRE.

—linkedin classes—for instance, photography business & marketing or freelance graphic and web designers

—relevant subreddits—such as r/webdev or r/freelancewriters

—growthhackers—to your marketing-minded

—relevant facebook classes—such as this wordpress this or one user encounter group

Participate in forums which are relevant for you and your experience. Provide recommendations, and join with other individuals.

Key takeaway: actually should you reside in a remote place, there's absolutely not any excuse to not connect with other people in your area.

11. Position yourself as a professional

There are ways you can set you as an authority in your area which goes beyond the conventional blog (that it feels like everybody has, nowadays).

For example, you could compose an ebook. The simple fact is anybody could print a book on amazon or in their with a stage such as gumroad...although not everybody understands that.

Besides showing your experience the subject available, composing an ebook provides you a reason to do speaking engagements or interviewsbecause you may speak on your new novel!

But if you are not a lot of a author, you are able to do anything else to place yourself as a professional, for example:

—produce an internet course—in your own, or even on a stage such as udemy or even skillshare

—construct another sort of information product—such as a bundle of snacks (movies, documents, etc..)

—mentor novices into the area online or in person (you can do this either on your computer or through a structured application)

Beyond devoting yourself as an specialist on the specified subject, ebooks and data products are just another means to create a little additional revenue.

Key takeaway: produce material which goes past the blog article. Educate others via ebooks and other sorts of information solutions. Require ryan robinson's instance, and you may also earn a little additional cash while on it.

In the long run, it is about relationship construction

Landing new customers does not need to be an intimidating task that occupies hours of valuable timeand you do not need to be more pushy or invest money on advertisements.

When it boils down to this, getting work for a freelancer is about building connections (offline or online) and demonstrating your own worth and experience. Take advantage of these approaches of passive marketing and you might begin daily with a few more mails in your email address.

# Chapter three: How to market yourself and find client as a freelancer

## 5 measures for landing your client as a freelancer

You get a well-defined approach, you might discover that landing your very first customer is much simpler than you envisioned. Following that, it is merely an issue of keeping them happy and locating more.

1. Construct and maintain a site

As a freelancer, then you clearly need to place yourself on the market. This means getting your services and work readily found on the internet.

Unless your initial customer comes to you out of a personal recommendation, then they are likely to find you via a search engine such as google. Have a look at this a-z guide to constructing your own site and start 1 now, if you do not already have you.

Your site must let visitors be conscious of your services and abilities, in addition to showcase your work and accomplishments. It also ought to maintain a continuous development—which means regularly upgrading your portfolio, keeping a site, and adding into a 'testimonials' section.

Aim to become personable yet professional when composing your site's copy. Heal yourself as the only real product which you're—your site ought to be filled with positive, enthusiastic and perceptive info.

On the topic of websites, be certain your site has a clearly defined goal and leadership. There is no use in composing winding sites about the great walk which you took throughout the park another day. You're attempting to be hired as a specialist for a specific provider, and your site needs to demonstrate your attention on and comprehension of the market.

Keep a professional-looking portfolio to prove you understand how to convert customer's thoughts into high quality projects. It is possible to create one having a committed host website like employ an illustrator that is independent to your site. If you do not have a thing to exhibit nonetheless, do the very best thing and include an downloadable resume to your site.

2. Network like mad

Frequently when it comes to hammering your way for a freelancer, you want to create friends to become successful. Speak to successful salespeople at precisely the exact same business or market as youpersonally, and inquire how they have started. Send them emails, even in case you do not know them, and kindly ask their tips on how to locate customers. Odds are, they will remember what it is like to be on your shoes and also be pleased to help out.

If you are wondering how to locate these successful salespeople, consider looking for a number of the more effective freelancer portfolios/sites. While you're there, have a look at their customer list and also do a tiny different brainstorming exercise. With this, I suggest sitting down having a bit of newspaper and asking yourself these questions:

- Why did this customer hire that freelancer?
- How can they make first contact that freelancer?
- Is it feasible they still require work from a different freelancer that offer a comparable service?

If the reply to the last query is yes, you always have the option to begin after the customer on twitter, join together on linkedin or just reach them out through email to let them know you're a freelance practitioner who accomplishes their work and would love to get connected with their business.

You would be surprised how successful this easy strategy is when it has to do with bettering your system and obtaining new contacts into your address book. Of course, if you email anyone in'freelancer manner' you need to add an email signature linking to a site, portfolio and applicable social networking accounts. Odds are, if you excite the individual's curiosity, they will look it over.

Also intention to participate in dwell twitter talks or media events both offline and online. These events can allow you to gain more visibility within your area.

3. Update your own linkedin profile

Linkedin is among the finest ways to find new customers as a freelancer. Since recruiters frequently search for freelance professionals in linkedin, it is a goldmine of chances.

Dedicate a day or weekend to ensuring your profile is polished and up-to-date. Make sure you have chosen the option that says 'receptive to new opportunities'. Add any appropriate info or uploads into a profile which you feel will help you bring new customers.

Do not forget to add a fantastic profile image, a career goal or ability outline, and attribute endorsements from other people on your community.

Utilize your present contacts, for example fellow classmates, workers, and other salespeople at precisely the exact same area to raise your community (both offline and online). The 'folks you will know' attribute on linkedin is a fantastic way to discover prospective customers and collaborators. It is also possible to have a look at your competitor's connections.

4. Collaborate with other people

Whether your alliance takes the type of guest blogging or posting to another site, or building your portfolio up by simply performing a free work for a friend or friend, do everything you can to get your name on the market along with your job printed... In exchange for referrals and testimonials.

Guest posting might not cover your invoices but it might catch the note of possible customers, especially in the event that you write to get a site with a great deal of traffic and authority. Make sure that the caliber of your guest article is large and reflects your specialist knowledge of a specific market area.

Considering that the grade is more critical than the amount, make sure you include infographics, pictures, illustrations and videos to produce your content additional engaging and relevant. This will inspire folks to realize your articles (and by extension, your freelance services) as precious.

While you may be wondering why, if your purpose is to be viewed as beneficial, you'd get the job done for free to get a friend or friend, but operating free of charge originally could be very a smart strategy on your freelance career. That is because everything you find as 'complimentary' additional men and women watch as a 'favor'. And individuals return favors.

For instance, if you woke up a symbol for a buddy who cannot afford to hire someone to do it (and you also do a fantastic job), their success becomes your achievement as each time they get a compliment on it, and they are very likely to mention by name. If somebody is happy with your job, they will almost always be pleased to spread the word about who is responsible, and you are able to increase your portfolio.

Additionally, there are a myriad of ways in that to unite the media I spoke about before with the idea of working at no cost to create maximum freelancer opportunities for you. Let us say that you email the articles direct to get an electronic manufacturer to (and humbly) figure out you discovered a couple of typos in a recent blog article. They will probably be thankful and thank you for the attention. Together with the first contact already cared for, you can use this chance to compose a followup email stating that you are looking to intern or volunteer to get a company like theirs while you receive your freelance business moving.

Collaborating with recognized brands and other specialists is among the smartest things you could do as a freelancer at the first phases of your career.

5. Be busy on social networking

This does not only mean facebook, twitter and linkedin. This means niche-specific social networking platforms which are utilized by professionals in your area of experience.

For instance, if you're a designer, then then establish a profile behance. If you're a programmer, utilize github. If you're a videographer, use vimeo. And so on.

Update your profiles relevant social networking accounts and exhibit your very best work to a targeted social networking crowd. Know your weaknesses and strengths, and play with them. 99 percent of the time, customers aren't likely to drop into your lap. They'll contact you via third party websites or via a friend or via your site.

Ensure you're putting your best foot forwards in this accessible universe of ours and handle social networking platforms as a sort of digital business card.

Additionally you may want to combine any applicable professional organisations (such as aiga for designers) and institutions (such as the freelancers union) to fulfill even more business peers and understand how others have located their achievement.

Locating your first customer as a freelancer does not need to be a challenging procedure: all you have to do is approach it using a open and collaborative mindset, and also a very clear awareness of your targets and aims.

Speak to as many individuals as you can—you will never know where your next customer will come out of. Think of what you would like your prospective customers and clients to view and place it front and centre on your site. Identify the kinds of customers you'd love to make use of and study how they generally go about locating builders.

Initially, target for only a handful of customers. If you keep up a positive mindset and a community-minded method of building your organization, you will have over a dozen before you even know it.

The best way to advertise yourself and locate customers as a freelancer

Let us face it freelancers the biggest challenge is to discover customers and promote yourselves.

If you are only getting started then it's likely that you don't have any clue how to find new customers or even get your name out there facing the ideal individuals.

While the task of finding customers and marketing your freelance business can seem very hard, it is in factn't, as long as you discover the proper platforms to perform that.

First—limit your target market:

Who are you looking to aim? It's very critical that you understand who actually your crowd is in connection with your freelance job. The majority of the salespeople at brainsfeed we encounter are unable to establish their target audience that likewise causes us as a stage hard to hook them up using the ideal jobs.

You can specify your market with what type of customers you'd love to work together or which kind of job you like doing the most.

Secondly—entire your profile all freelancers platforms and also create your profile stand out:

While viewing over literally tens of thousands of profile, we have seen a huge 70% salespeople with finished profiles bringing companies and projects compared to the ones with incomplete or half profiles.

Be sure to use every element of your profile to showcase your own abilities, let us face it a customer who would be paying for a job will do his study you before going forward, a finished profile builds more confidence in an internet world.

Emphasize your very best work at the profile and list any certificates if any.

Third—be anywhere:

Produce accounts with significant societal networks ( linkedin, facebook, google, quora, twitter), guest post on channels and blogs, that also enables you to achieve better search results on google and assist to make your new identity. You would be amazed the amount of followers and prospects you are going to get when you've yourself on a broad variety of websites throughout the internet.

Brainsfeed has helped achieve a great deal of its franchisees create quite a few leads from assisting them tweak their own societal profiles on the stage.

Freelance marketing suggestions:

- The very first step to advertise yourself as a excellent freelancer is to
  seek out a means to interest your intended market and bring them

and also the ideal means to do that's to reach out into a outer and inner circle, showcase a while in your social networking stations and a construct a portfolio to showcase the abilities you've got.

- Among the best tactics to secure more customers to your kitty is to become online freelancer platforms such as upwork, brainsfeed and lots of more.

We all know how exhausting it is to become missing from the crowded platforms consequently we made brainsfeed, brainsfeed makes you visible to all of the customers onboard and doesn't request undesirable files aside from the fundamentals, brainsfeed will be and will remain a restricted and curated platform for both salespeople, so you get to fit and also reach out into the relevant customers without being missing.

- You will find sites and programs that enable you to guest article, share whatever you know! Proceed to discussion and answer a few questions or answer to site comments. This enables you to seem to be an authority in the topic and boost your credibility on the internet.

Another fantastic way is to make little quick videos on the topic and release online on several different platforms.

- Obtaining referrals, there's nothing more powerful than having somebody advocating your name and solutions, referrals will be the very important part to get a freelancer and also they are not difficult for you.

# 6 points to learn about getting freelance customers

The internet is an infinite sea of possibilities. You may select your own experience, working in a design service or as in-house designer. You can begin your own site or know the craft of 3d utilizing online blender tutorials. Or you may do something much more daring—split all on your own.

However, being a different designer implies that you also must be a business man. You cannot tune from the nitty gritty of contracts and ledgers. If you do, then your company will not take off. It is an essential evil.

01. Enjoy your customers

Whether you are a self explanatory designer or a company owner, you are going to be enthusiastic about your service or product, or you are likely to be enthused about the people that you serve.

It is even more significant for self-evident designers to appreciate their customers over their resources, than it will be for a number of different kinds of business proprietor. The main reason is that: the style world goes so quickly, and also design tendencies change so fast, it requires fire to maintain. That surroundings breeds enthusiasm for the craft—and rightly so! Don't forget to channel all of that fire and vitality back in your clientele.

Make customers feel confident on your skills by demonstrating them excitement

When company is positioned just like that, it is a lot more palatable to your designer. How do you help more individuals? How do you leverage your design skills to create more of an effect on your clientele? How do you reach people to produce an effect for?

02. Be cautious about your providers

Step one in getting somebody's company is to be more clear on which you provide. There is no space for vagueness and uncertainty. 1 approach to guarantee you're conveying that which you provide is to understand what you are best at and what value you bring to this table.

First of all, you will need to examine your marketplace. Learn about who is playing on your area, and who is satisfying their clientele. What sells well? What markets of the marketplace are not being served as completely as many others?

**FREELANCE CONSULTING: PROVIDE SERVICES TO HIGH TICKET CUSTOMERS. BUILD AND GROW YOUR OWN GIG EMPIRE.**

Up to now, try to think as if your prospective customers. The longer spent exploring from the opinion of a potential, the further you are going to place where these prospects might be served.

You should also search for opportunities on the marketplace. Maybe there is a specific market that gets less support since it isn't'cool'. Or perhaps your competition is not communication in a manner your marketplace knows. Perhaps you're capable of teaching prospects. Or perhaps you provide more value than they're doing.

But establishing is not enough. You need to be aware of the distinction between what you are doing, and also exactly what the customer receives. As an instance,'we do character development' means nothing to the majority of customers,' where'raising conversion rates from targeting demographics individually' generally makes more sense.

Home depot sells clients'drills'. The clients need'a hole in their wall'. Same thing, different language.

Some customers will be curious to know what type of drill you're going to be using, and you think that it's the very best drill to the job. All customers will want to learn whether you're planning to provide them the specific hole that they desire.

03. Ensure you stand outside

Everybody who is fighting to get a bit of the customer pie claims they are good. And you are likely to need to cut through this sound and then stand out.

To create unique, you will need to think about: what makes you unique, the best way to pitch which into prospectives, the best way to market this, and the way you place yourself as a professional.

And if everybody is saying exactly the same thing, it becomes trickier.

Back prior to responsive internet design was something, I recall promoting responsive web layout to prospects. It was just like magic, and if combined with the remainder of our provide it had been the icing on the cake. Nowadays, responsive design is not a nicety, but also a requirement. The job might nonetheless be precious, but when everybody else is also doing this, the magic has been missing.

You can get round this by performing the subsequent:

Use testimonials from the customers to add believability to your site

- Add the case research to your website, highlighting the way you solved a specific issue.
- Use testimonials from previous customers on your website.
- Maintain your skills clean—keep together with the newest trends and techniques.
- Play to your strengths: consider what you're able to offer that others do not.

04. Take an abysmal process

When you draw a potential customer, you will need to get a crystal clear on-boarding procedure.

Prospects become customers when they are convinced in you, your own capacity to deliver outcomes and your value proposition. A good procedure will truly help you instil this assurance.

An on boarding process can help place new customers at ease

Likewise decreasing customers that you really do not think will enable you to deliver outcomes or your own value proposition to is both significant.

Maybe they need something you have no idea how to do (and it is sufficiently from your wheelhouse for one to find out in a timely fashion). Or maybe their funding is too little. Perhaps the product they are selling does not align with you.

At any of these instances, it is your function to close the bargain down, instead of compromising your ethics or integrity by providing bad building or work lousy products.

**FREELANCE CONSULTING: PROVIDE SERVICES TO HIGH TICKET CUSTOMERS. BUILD AND GROW YOUR OWN GIG EMPIRE.**

While we are talking about tripping the bargain right down, there are a couple of things to keep an eye out for. Ensure...

- They possess the money to devote to working together with you personally, or at least to begin.
- They are ready prepared to begin work on the job shortly.
- Your characters can work nicely together.
- They honor you, your own job, along with your own rate.
- They have enthusiasm for their project.

While it might be tempting to choose any work which comes your way, you do not wish to place yourself in a gloomy situation. You will need to be certain you wish to work with a person as far as they would like to work together with you.

05. Create a fantastic contract

You likely know you will want great contracts set up before you do business with other businesses. For much more about creating acceptable contracts, take a look at our post about the 10 contract that you ought to know about.

A fantastic contract will shield you against customers who do not need to cover

However, the best contract in the world might not assist you if somebody on the opposing side of earth decides to vanish without paying.

Have great deals, have apparent payment tips, and be sensible about that which you're doing business with.

For instance, simple but in depth contract files that summarize when we anticipate every partial payment, before every bit of work beginning, so we may be paid as work is finished. No payment details operate best for the niche, put it in writing, just in the event of.

As depressing as it may sound, I had advocate cleaning upon which the procedures have been on your state and country to matters such as small claims courts and set bureaus. Hopefully you will not ever want, however focusing on just how to establish the procedure for motion if a person violates the principles will provide you the confidence to tackle issues suitably, as opposed to shying away.

06. Keep tabs on your hours

Would you understand just how long your preceding endeavors took you? The length of time can you devote to each portion of the procedure? In the event that you should simply take a particular section of the plan function, how do influence the purchase price?

With this information, you are screwing yourself as well as your wallet. The greater you track your own time and effort, the more accurate your quotes become. Become an expert time-tracker.

There is plenty of excellent job management applications available, however they'll just be effective as the individual with themchoose an instrument and understand it.

# Ten ways of get customers when you are getting started

Initially, goal to the only a couple of customers. An individual may possibly be fortune along with perhaps a family friend (thanks mom!). A couple of customers means you've created a base of individuals who will provide you money for your own expertise. And as much, you've heard what worked regarding landing those customers, and that means it's possible to use exactly the exact methods over and over.

Listed below are a couple of ideas on how best to get those very first few customers:

1. Give your take in a preexisting item

This is particularly useful to get designers. Re-design a favorite internet site with your very own distinct take, and explain exactly why you've made the changes you've made. You may see a few examples here, here, and also here.

Which site if you re design? Focus to a niche site the form of client that you would like to get hired by uses essentially the absolute most.

Illustration for post titled an experienced freelancers guide to finding customers

Why do so? A couple of reasons: first, you've bending your chops as developer to exhibit your abilities to both the peers and possible customers. Secondly, you are revealing you have specific thoughts to produce somebody else's business easier. Third, you are creating the sort of job you would like, dependent on the personality and form of client.

2. Utilize job boards

Take to we work remotely, legitimate jobs, smashing jobs, e-lance, krop, as well as fiverr. Initially, eventually become a fire hose of pitches. Lead with resolving their own problem and never minding about your abilities. If you are beginning and only plain want that the job, then bid about whatever even when it's less than that which you would like to produce. Every one's gotkindly start someplace.

Why do so? After you begin you do not a enormous network. Giving an answer for as many projects as possible gets your portfolio and name at the front of as many people as you possibly can. Even in the event that you devote a couple minutes before responding to a bill to master a little about the provider, you'll be miles ahead of every one. If you listen from the firm and also they do not hire one, ask whether it's possible to keep intouch base. That is beneficial if they've future job or even the others that they are able to refer you around.

3. Use your present contacts

Fellow awakened classmates? Employees from exactly the area you interned? Other salespeople you have established some connection with? Send short and individual e mails to everyone else you know, telling them exactly what exactly are you currently searching for, and immediately describing the sort of customers you are trying to find. You may also provide them a"finders fee" in case their guide lands give you a gig.

Mention what you do especially, where they could realize work samples, and also the kind of customers you're searching for. Be brief, also make it effortless for them to say with a lien charge.

4. Speak to other free-lancers on your field

These individuals are not always your contest—they truly are your community. Introduce yourself. Once you set a little bit of attachment, provide to assist them pick up their idle if they are too busy to deal with their own workload. There are an infinite number of networking events on the web and also in real existence. A fantastic solution to create relations with industry peers will be always to demonstrate how helpful you're.

Where would you locate them? Social media, media events, professional associations (such as aiga for designers) and institutions (just like the freelancers union). In the event that you went into school for that which you are urinating in, then stay in contact with classmates. And stay in contact with past colleagues.

Speak to successful salespeople in your business and get them specific questions regarding how they receive the task they perform. The speedy question mail technique is just a excellent solution to really get your foot in the doorway too. You get yourself a fantastic bit of information out of a freelancer that knows their own shit, you turn into a blip on the radar, and also you're seen by these as someone who would like to study on their website, and less some body begging for the work.

5. Learn where the folks you wish to work with saving their time

Networking events? On the web communities? See themto all those places and start conversations. Quite helpful, not pushy or sales-y.

6. Create diverse content and make yourself known

You are not a writer in case you are not writing. You are not really a photographer if you are simply looking for fancy camera gear. But a lot more than simply working in your own craft, you're able to begin a site, a podcast, or even perhaps a youtube station to make a name for yourself. Too many salespeople focus their articles in their industry—create content which benefits your possible customers.

· some thing that you need every customer might know more about the sort of job that you do.

· if customers require the very same things (i.e. Make the logo bigger) and so they're the wrong questions to ask, so what do you teach them about the ideal questions to ask?

· exactly what exactly are several quick repairs customers can make with your own business enterprise, primarily based on your own expertise?

· what are several success stories or case studies out of work you've achieved?

· what tools will you talk clients? What novels can be urge?

7. Start at no cost

Free job gets a bad rap, however if you are just beginning, occasionally it's crucial to construct your portfolio and also pursue some opportunity you can get. Working free of charge will be a good deal more viable if you at work which pays, at which you may certainly do it on the other side.

Working free of charge is catchy, however has it's set. You've got to cautious and tactical when employed by nothing. However, if you are attempting to land your very first freelance gig, then you have gotta do exactly what you've gotta perform. Keep this advice in mind when minding free job:

- If you're doing a job at no cost, ensure the customer realizes they're hiring you for the own vision and expertise. Only since the job is free does not indicate your expertise and experience must not be contemplated.
- Speak to your customer prior to the job starts about potentially having some referrals once the job is completed, simply because they will certainly be content with your job (make certain that this is happens!). Additionally make sure you request a testimonial out of their store once the project is completed.

- Inform them exactly what your "ordinary" speed is and inform them that when they truly are happy about the outcome, you are more than delighted to utilize them or to get fresh endeavors in that speed.
- If you're doing work at no cost, make certain it's from the niche that you wish to complete more work and it's really the form of client and job that you desire to complete greater work for.

Absolutely free work, at the lack of discovering paying customers, also can take the kind of unwanted projects or individual projects. These can become considered a wonderful showcase of one's abilities and vision.

8. Create a helpful product

If you are a writer, make a manual that assists your form of customers create content that is better. If you are a designer, then write a one-of-a-kind which explains how designers may produce the job run smoother. If you are a programmer, develop a quick program which helps people accomplish an activity faster. The services and products can be purchased, however if you are beginning, provide them away at no cost. Create a contact training course, a printable pdf, a web program.

Why do so? If you can construct something of significance, folks will begin to use it and referring to it. If you create something which directly affects the form of people that you are interested in being appreciated, they'll notice you like doing a favor with all the goods and understand your name.

Take these examples: " my buddy nate kontny created draft, an easy writing tool. Brennan dunn created just a tiny research to demonstrate how much annually arming your hourly rate could bring about (and he's got an item available for sale too). Tina roth eisenberg is therefore very good at creating products such as tattly, teuxdeux, also creative mornings, she does not have to accomplish client work.

9. Locate a free-lancing partner

Locate a freelancer that works at a related discipline together with skills that enhance your own personal and see whether you may work together on a few projects. Designer? Partner along with a programmer to offer you a larger solution. Writer? Partner up with a designer which means you're able to write the articles.

10. Make a set of who you intend to work with

Possessing a welldefined market makes it more straightforward to source prospects out. Spending some time daily researching businesses which fit the profile. Introduce them. Even when they do not hire one, they know your name. How will you decide on a niche to concentrate on? Think of these questions:

- What industry can you actually utilize services and products out of or enjoy?
- What industry hires salespeople with abilities such as yours?
- What industry do you like networking in and being part of?

# Chapter four: Build and grow your personal gig empire

## 9 surefire tactics to boost your freelance business

If you are coming out of our informative article:how to establish your free-lancing business at 10 days, and then you are well on your path to building your property.

You may now have several regular customers that are keeping you grounded, or simply you've yet to find yourself a client to remain the dotted line, whether you might have one or two hundred customers almost always there is room to develop and build bridges.

It is at this stage you are likely wondering how you're able to kick start your business to over drive and target the customers you want to sustain your own particular lifestyle.

Well, wonder no further! To be certain you begin this new year with a bang, and we've assembled 9 sure fire techniques you may use to cultivate your outsourcing company.

Without further ado, let us get directly to it

1. Define your own strengths and flaws.

Whether you are new into the biz or in case you happen to be operating for a little while, it's amazing to have sometime out to investigate your successes and failures of this year. Begin by assessing your procedures, evaluating your highs and lows, and also make a concrete collection of what's worked well for you so much, and also what's not.

Remember: great empires are constructed from info, datadata therefore your current stats are golden for the own expansion. Can you accomplish your targets? Does your site have the traffic you've intended for? Can you can follow your own budgets and so are you on course to make it to the actions points on your business strategy?

Certainly one of the very basic approaches to grow would be to rid yourself of things which hold you backagain. Which is anything from poor internal approaches to adverse customs, thus a comprehensive analysis during this period is paramount to a impending development.

Start looking for ways you can make sure that failures do not replicate themselvesand means that you can make certain your successes perform. If you should be not able to be objective on your business, it'd be valuable to get help from a company analyst that could have the relevant skills essential to identify which areas will need to improve.

2. Review your own rates.

At the start of any enterprise, rates are generally put down of inexperience and fear your visitors will probably be delay in the event that you charge a great deal. Once you are established, a summary of one's rates will make certain you are charging appropriately to the value you are contributing for your clientele.

Move away by charging an hourly rate speed for the own time and focus on everything you are bringing to the clients' dining table. As soon as you've now been operating for a little while, you will have a whole lot more confidence to learn that if an individual does not appreciate your value, your time will be spent on a client who will. Compare to the regional competitions, are the pricing arrangements and offers similar, or will there be some thing you can include to earn your service or product a great deal more attracting the marketplace? Constant report on those rates you're giving to prospective customers, in contrast to exactly what your competition do, is likely to be certain you're always earning the maximum money for every single potential endeavor.

3. Improve your abilities.

There is no uncertainty that the lengthier you are supplying something, the higher you get at it. Combine this onthejob adventure with professional development; and also chances to learn and study from governments on your industry who've already hauled later on that you are on.

Run a present abilities audit you and any staff which are free-lancing under your roof and also evaluate every one the strengths and flaws of these individuals. Employ any recommendations produced in reviews from the existing and previous customers, and really carry aboard any information offered to you from people who used your services. It is possible to even attempt one-on-one training to get started.

The further your abilities enhance, the more more dependable you will become in your specialty and the further your product will likely maintain popular that may provide you with the selection of one's clientele.

4. Increase your offering.

In case you started your freelancer business by simply offering a couple of services, to cultivate you have to enlarge your approach. It will not suggest that you want to understand new abilities, however it will mean you want to do the job with those around you. If you are a graphic designer collaborate with a professional to offer you a whole package to your clientele. If you are a webdesigner increase your offering by dealing together with an seo strategist.

You will find a whole host of freelancer professionals around freelancer.com that possess the abilities and accessibility necessary to help your company grow.

5. Expand your promotion strategy.

Nevertheless your advertising plan began, it might continually be enlarged. Increase your presence to social networking or think of a direct email effort. If you aren't certain how to start out, place a advertisement for an advertising professional who'll have the ability to reevaluate your previous effects and create recommendations to upcoming campaigns. Bear in mind, you may always get more and more creative to enlarge the range of one's merchandise. Start thinking beyond this box.

Social networking is essential to the expansion of your freelancer business and no matter what period of your outsourcing profession you are at, you could do more! There are always chances to create brand new followers, research fresh programs and also you have the ideal chance to proceed viral in order for the articles reaches on the other areas of earth. A fantastic social-media strategist will generate new sales leads, and may allow you to down the way to greater visibility to you along with your own product.

Active social networking direction is probably one of the utmost truly effective keys to unlock the doorway to a larger market, and you're able to participate with a specialist.

6. Build strong relationships.

Safe connections are critical to the long-term achievement of your freelance business enterprise. Build robust, longterm relationships with your present customers to ensure they consistently go back for you whenever they will have a demand for the goods, and also consult with your own coworkers. Speak to your entire current and previous clients regularly.

With the electronic era committing us exactly the planet at our hands, it's crucial that you'think locally' and be sure relationships with those organizations in front doorstep are bullet proof. It's those individuals you may see for a catchup to permit them to have to understand and esteem you personally in order they are able to pass your details for their clientele.

You have to start small when building relationships however watch as time passes the way they are able to contribute to your growth and success globally.

You must construct powerful relationships with your providers and people that are spent on your freelance business enterprise. Not only will this make sure that the procedures are more efficient, however in addition, it means you will truly have a support system that'll encourage your professional and personal growth.

7. Network.

When conducting a freelance company, also you may believe that media isn't vital. It's.

Networking, both offline and on, is probably one of the very vital things you can perform in order to make sure the development of your small business. It's imperative that you can know the others in your niche who're your competitor or your own service so you will be in a situation to benefit from available opportunities.

While it can be tempting to concentrate on internet forums just (where you are right, these are tremendously favorable), it's vital for the wellbeing and future growth you simply leave the convenience of one's working environment and exhibit your business in circles that are applicable. Liven your organization with a fantastic modern business-card and also subscribe for seminars and conventions in your specialty.

Have you got one?

There is a straightforward way: hire a graphic designer to generate one for you personally. In this manner, you may make sure your small business card ends up on-top of the heap.

8. Get ready yourself to outsource.

In case you have been flying for awhile, the idea of growing and handing more control of almost any region of one's freelancer company may be somewhat daunting. We are around. If you would like to enlarge your company to a bigger thing, together with world wide customers, benefiting from additional hands-on deck is indispensable.

There is no requirement to outsource every thing at one time. Start small and participate by a virtual assistant, or even perhaps a book keeper who are able to take control some of those bigger but more timeconsuming tasks. Once you are familiar with that, then consider additional job it's possible to handover. If you're not well prepared to share with you the responsibility of one's freelancer business, then it's not possible that you cultivate. You're merely a single man with a restricted quantity of hours on daily and should you try to get it done, you are going to burnout and wont have the ability to reap someone of the huge benefits that running a booming freelancer company brings.

Get at the top of the today, and also you may let's after.

9. Focus on longterm endeavors.

If you're looking for work, provide your providers in a continuous basis. The shortterm projects are best for keeping cashflow moving, however it could be the bigger projects that can bring one of the maximum experience in the region and may even provide room for growth on your abilities and development.

Obviously, you do not simply'get' long-term endeavors. The duration of your job is something which may be negotiated by demonstrating your values and also showcasing your valuable competencies. For each and every job that you are given, think longterm and decide exactly what you're able to provide your customer to keep your relationship, and also flow of job, steady.

# Create your job: 10 strategies for being a high-paid freelancer

The freelancer market is flourishing and there really are a whole lot of opportunities, specially in the event that you get proficient at boosting yourself and building an electronic portfolio.

What I like best about free-lancing is it is a simple and inexpensive situation to enter and it works great as a negative hustle as you continue to be in school, or even save additional money whilst working out a fulltime job.

Typically, you do not automatically need to really have a university level to acquire well-paid outsourcing work because salespeople are hired more to get his or her private new and electronic portfolio compared to their credentials or resume.

Given you will probably be free-lancing in 1 manner or another all through your livelihood, you could too begin building your own personal brand and identifying yourself currently from the highly-competitive market for superior freelance job.

The information about your emerging freelance economy:

# FREELANCE CONSULTING: PROVIDE SERVICES TO HIGH TICKET CUSTOMERS. BUILD AND GROW YOUR OWN GIG EMPIRE.

The information shows that freelancing is increasingly getting the trail millennials follow to find work experience and also"make" their particular tasks:

1. Almost 50 percent of millennial employees happen to be free-lancing (upwork)

2. 43 percent of this u.s. Work force will probably be free-lancers by 2020 (nasdaq).

3. 6-1% of freelancers focus in two to three presents (slash workers).

4. 82 percent of distant employees reported lower pressure levels and high morale (pgi).

5. Artificial intelligence, development hacking, machine learning, insta-gram promotion, ios/android development and new strategy would be the freelancer skills in highest demand in 20-19 (really).

6. 63 percent of salespeople from the u.s. Say they favor their own work-from-home livelihood on a conventional occupation (upwork/ freelancers union)

7. Most salespeople think their livelihood is more stable and also they will have more leverage compared to the usual conventional day occupation only because they've a diversified portfolio of customers as opposed to the usual job with one company. (upwork/freelancers union)

The best way to produce your job:

The basis of longterm achievement like a freelancer is now creating a distinguishing own brand.

This means you want a definite and succinct narrative of that you have, the financial value of this expertise you give to additional and everything makes you apart from every one else with a very similar freelancer skill-set.

Google is your newest desktop computer test thus remember that hiring managers and small business people hiring to get a searchable freelancer gig are sure to investigate you by assessing your name.

This means you have to cultivate a personal brand using a professional-looking site and also a electronic portfolio that shows your job experience and the manner in which you receive results for those that you utilize.

This is how you avoid getting a commodity in an independent job market-place like upwork. Even in case you develop a portfolio within those market places, you are going to still require a professional-looking internet site to flaunt your own freelancer job.

Listed below are 10 of the greatest hints for becoming a high-value freelancer on the internet:

1. Define your own personal brand and name your small business

First thing you are going to need is a company name. In the event you are usually the person doing the job, then it's probably a fantastic plan to brand yourself and utilize your name.

When you've defined your name, you should enroll it as an domainname, ideally employing some blend of words which finishes. Com or.me.

2. Brand yourself with your own personal personal site

Next, you are going to need a professional-looking internet site that definitely informs the narrative of that you are, what you offer and you are very different.

You'll be up and running in less than two hours using a internet site having an affordable wordpress host and also a wordpress theme template. I detail how exactly to do so within my own 5-part totally free video training which branding guide about building your own personal brand and electronic portfolio.

3. Build an electronic portfolio which demonstrates work

# FREELANCE CONSULTING: PROVIDE SERVICES TO HIGH TICKET CUSTOMERS. BUILD AND GROW YOUR OWN GIG EMPIRE.

Once your site is on the internet, you should begin building an electronic portfolio which features case studies which reveal the outcomes that you've achieved for the customers in the kind with the 3-part arrangement:

1. Problem: the company challenge undergone.

2. Solution: the plan and also tactics you invented and executed.

3. Results: the quantifiable consequences with metrics for that which you've really achieved.

In case you do not have some freelancer customers still, you may need to supply your professional services at a reduction initially for more experience. Your portfolio is vital for getting a high-value freelancer.

4. Boost your linkedin profile for hunt

It's also very important that you simply have an energetic presence on linked in and also a highly-optimized linked in profile therefore recruiters and hiring managers earnestly searching for salespeople will get one in the search outcome.

Additionally, your linkedin profile is a very good possibility to say that the associations you might be part of, your own volunteer experience also to provide testimonials from the clientele and previous managers entirely on your own profile.

5. Build your personal after on social networking

There is a huge quantity of chances which may be gained by building an expert societal networking presence on face book, twitter or even youtube.

Utilize your personal profile as well as create another small business page to talk about your expertise and make a relationship by engaging having an internet audience that could take advantage of the expertise and expertise.

6. Acquire more experience quick with on the web free-lancing market places

In case you do not possess a great deal of experience, you should begin building your abilities and expertise with bidding low freelance gigs at a freelancer market place including upwork.

These freelance marketplaces supply a fantastic place to seek out your first jobs to get paid testimonials from and develop your portfolio.

7. Secure an online payments account along with also a financial administration tool

In case you are not planning to utilize freelancer market places, you're able to accept payments at a professional manner from the customers through pay pal or stripe.

They bill just a 2.9% commission on the sum paid and $0.30 on each trade. To handle finances, issue bills and quantify your own regular monthly cashflow the application usage is either quickbooks or even and.co (affiliate link).

8. Utilize time tracking software on manage your free-lancing gigs and billable hours

To optimize your earnings as a free-lancers attempting to sell your time per summertime, you have to concentrate on tracking and raising your billable hours per week.

To build your own project as a well-paid free-lancers (in the place of the usual poorly paid or completely insolvent freelancer, and this is significantly more prevalent than you believe), you should issue statements with a specific cost break down of precisely the way your customers money was spent in order to prevent any confusion.

9. Always sign legally-binding digital contracts with your customers

In case you are not working via a free-lancing internet site like upwork, that offers freelance contracts, so you always need to sign a legally-binding contract.

Contract law can be hard to enforce across boundaries nonetheless it is rather imperative that you will get written down precisely what you may do to help the client and just how far you may receive paid in exchange.

10. Think about incorporating your freelance business to save taxes

Many developed nations supply significant tax incentives to boost salespeople and tiny organizations to cultivate their organization and much better weather downturns.

If I work free of charge to get experience and exposure?

Surely not. Just do not. Never.

It disturbs me just how many men and women inform you who doing work at no cost can be considered a fantastic thing for the own career. It hastens your services directly from the beginning, giving customers (and yourself!)) the incorrect belief on what to anticipate. Plus, it infrequently provides you with some benefit chance to obtain experience than paid job will.

It is extremely very important not to misrepresent yourself. If you are fresh into the sport, do not feign for a larger company compared to the oneperson micro business you're. Do not claim to own skills you cannot backup, or you'll dig yourself into a pit. Be directly up and honest about your strengths and experience (or insufficient).

Most organizations just do not have the budget to pay for a seasoned practitioner for top-tier freelancer job, therefore they are prepared to have a punt on more economical in-experienced free-lancers—perhaps faculty students, recent grads, or even the latest career-switchers. Should you represent yourself frankly, and clarify that your low speed is reflective of your own lack of business expertise, and they'll understand exactly what they're becoming and what exactly to anticipate. Should you do ultra-professionally, you're dismiss off their low expectations from the water, also acquire a longterm client that'll help gain grip.

Afterward, as you gain experience and confidence with every new job, re-asses if you provide enough additional value to justify an interest speed increase (or experimentation with different pricing techniques) for another project.

Do so: investigate what additional neighborhood noob tasks pay in your town. You wish to start off charging significantly more than the usual low-skilled hamburger flipper, however perhaps not quite around an experienced expert with years of working experience on your own industry. The way you price your services has got a tremendous psychological effect on what your customers perceive your own value. Price yourself that you're respected, nevertheless, you still come around being a bargain as a result of your lack of experience. Giving away your time at no cost accomplishes nothing.

Starting small is best

In case you are at a part time or full-time job today—or you are students—you are at the ideal spot to get started freelancing. Jumping into fulltime sourcing out of nothing is actually a jolt. It requires a while to develop a clientele, specially in the event that you have not previously grown a system of relations to telephone up on.

Twice as far as you can from the existing employer. Learn their job management procedure. Discover how they talk to customers and manage balances. Make a sponge that are able to consume all of those encouraging business skills which are valuable once you are outside in your own like a freelancer.

Start freelancing with one little job at one time across the medial side. As soon as I started off as a university student I just worked around 5 hours each week in my very first job. My client knew what he had been becoming, and he had been really happy to offer students some experience in market for slower, more economical work.

After that tasks done, undertake still another. Why not a marginally tougher one this moment. Can be the confidence growing nonetheless? When you've experienced the procedure once, does this feel more natural that the 2nd, third, and fourth time round?

# FREELANCE CONSULTING: PROVIDE SERVICES TO HIGH TICKET CUSTOMERS. BUILD AND GROW YOUR OWN GIG EMPIRE.

Before you know it, you should have completed 5 or even 10 little job and you're going to feel just like you realize very well what this free-lancing item is about. (you wont know yet! But every tiny bit of confidence and experience can add up.)

Would you reside smoothly too?

It just will not happen that fast, for this reason, you have to put up yourself along with a few security to permit for a slow beginning.

Maybe not everybody may get that luxury. Imagine when you've got no choice except to call home somewhere pricey? Imagine if you currently have a family to support?

A lot of people advocate not becoming into outsourcing until you've stored up the same of 3—a few weeks wages (or living expenses) being a contingency"runway". Total service that idea. The most experienced salespeople who have learned just how to mitigate the freelancer roller-coaster of income that is inconsistent, could still have the strange slow spot that contributes to irregular earnings. You cannot be living pay check into pay check and live being a freelancer. It's not really consistent enough and you will worry out yourself until you've hardly gotten started.

Do that: create a strategy for how you can transition easily in the present location in to an independent life. Would you get started freelancing on both sides and just create the jump once you have built a little client-base and a number of savings like a seat? Would you set your living position to truly save cash in prep for irregular income since you gradually build your company? Speak with your parents, partner, or even some other relatives and buddies concerning ways that they could encourage you you never need to dive into the deep end.

Build reputation & relationships

That really is exactly what powerful freelancing is about. Even once you've already been doing this for years, this goal not varies.

The number 1 way to construct a sustainable, fulltime freelancer career is always to quality professional connections with satisfied customers who would like to refer you for their own friends and coworkers. Recommendations referrals are at which the very best work stems out of, as well as your oldest freelancer efforts ought to be aimed in generating these kinds of relationships.

That is why functioning on economical gig market places will not allow you to get quite far. The connections that you create you can find frequently unbiased trades which do not build any true standing beyond the un portable internal evaluations within those programs.

It is why functioning locally supplies you a far wider beginning. The standing you will build working closely together with companies in your area results in a trusting network of satisfied customers who is referrals take far more weight than people from random strangers.

Assembling a solid standing is easier than you may think. It all will take will be committing to to providing your client using as much significance as you may potentially offer, repeatedly on every job you need to do. In the event that you care about your customer's success, then do every thing in your ability to aid them reach, they'll observe those additional efforts and reward you with devotion and frequent referrals.

Therefore select customers that you simply can relate solely to. You wish to become building ventures, not merely doing tasks.

## Top tips to land your writing gig at freelancer

The elation—and possibly surprise—of landing your first writing gig can be actually a great experience! Specially if your very first gig may be the consequence of hard labour then one you've prepared for, then it's quite an achievement, and you also deserve a pat on your back!

To maintain yourself wellgrounded, it always may help to comprehend once you initially started pruning and the way you landed the first writing position. For those who have not begun freelancing or obtained a paid writing gig nonetheless, subsequently freelancer.com, then a jobsite for salespeople, is a great spot to get started.

What motivates buyers to freelancer.com?

Together with comparable job-sites such as elance.com and odesk.com, freelancer.com is still amongst the least difficult job internet sites to browse. All you have to do is enroll to get a freelancer.com accounts and register free of charge. As easily, you could even place your very first projects at no cost and bid from the remainder for a minor cost.

What brings authors to freelancer.com

On the author's character, it is s easy to set an account up. Simply enroll your username, then create a profile, and then navigate for endeavors. Without the prior onsite expertise, you are all set to bidding to your next writing project!

What authors ought to avert

The best thing about becoming a freelancer is you are self conscious. In line with all the freelancer.com's new avian logothat you are free like a bird! The sky's the limit because you like the conveniences and advantages of freelancer writing.

Freelance writing, nevertheless, comes with certain jobs and responsibilities. Should anyone ever aspire to land your first writing gig (rather perhaps not create it your own past), then build your livelihood on several things-to-do. Let us sum up them whilst the top tips to keep in mind while employed as a capable author on freelancer.com:

Hint number 1: do not procrastinate signing up. Register today!

Don't have any 2nd thoughts about registering to get a freelancer account. Because of jobsite, freelancer.com is still amongst the very legit internet sites for separate authors. This you are able to go right ahead and bid for shortterm contracts or to get longterm work.

Hint no 2: do not take your profile to get granted.

Make the most of your portfolio of credentials and qualifications by simply posting them onto your own profile. But, keep your data job-related rather than private, personal

Information.

Having a few exceptions, most authors are personal men and women. Ergo, should you like your privacy and don't have any intentions of giving it up, be favorable however keep professional.

Hint number 3: with no arrogance, take your qualifying tests.

Freelancer.com's examinations are somewhat more than rigid evaluations. If you should be up to this challenge, then they truly are fun methods of bettering your existing skills.

By way of example, freelancer.com provides qualifying exams which test your language proficiency and control of this speech. You'll also find assessments which judge your

Knowledge on rules for both companies and authors. You ought to just take these exams since they are going to appear on your freelancer.com portfolio.

Hint #4: do not bidding on every thing. Rather, be discerning!

Anxious as you're to property your first position, be discerning with your own bids. Being an independent contractor, don't hesitate to select your clientele. Afterall, it's merely a question of time till they choose one.

Remember: instinct will frighten one you did not escape from this "rat race" only to input the following dogeatdog world. Thus, by your

Personal criteria, try and out-wit the contest and out do yourself.

Hint #5: prevent becoming diverted. Continue to keep your eyes onto the dash board.

The dashboard is where you can track your messages and projects as they come. Meanwhile, pay attention to your own goals and soon you discover your specialty. This also contributes to a fine, clear break and also perhaps a very clear introduction to you.

Hint number 6: be unwilling to navigate for tasks on occasion. Do not stay idle!

While awaiting the busy bids to materialize, make an effort never to stagnate. Try to find much more

Jobs and scan the hottest projects which match your own specialty.

Hint number 7: do not overlook your overhead costs.

Before your initial payments begin coming in, perform a small bookkeeping. If your overhead costs are minimal at the moment, you ought to attempt to keep up a simple check and balance of expenses, for example monthly subscription fees.

Hint #8: avoid assuring supplies that sound too-good-to-be-true.

In accord with hint no 4, do not be scared to express"no more" to suspicious endeavors. Anywhere on the internet, you can encounter

Imbecile outsourcers who prey firsttimers and beginners.

To discover scams premature on, assess outsourcer's reviews. Get accustomed to current rates or levels to prevent yourself by being duped or duped to working for pennies.

Hint #9: prevent activities that get you suspended.

From the beginning, keep from any abuse on the work website. For example, freelancer.com restricts what you're able to post and the way it is possible to get intouch with your prospective companies.

In case freelancer.com does suspend your accounts, it is going to need days

To weeks prior to the job-site removes your suspension. This translates into lost a corrupt standing as it reflects in your own accounts.

Hint #10: do not quit advancing! Learn and develop.

To facilitate in to your initial writing gig, overcome your fears and insecurities. With constant exposure and exercise, you are able to slowly and surely build your own strengths, and enlarge your skills on many different topics.

To improve your comprehension, learn as much as possible and hear these pros. They may be the very first to inform you to not cease growing or

Improving your writing abilities.

# Chapter five: How to consult as a freelancer

## The way to be a top freelance consultant

However operate and well-paid work really are just two very different items. If you would like to turn into an experienced freelance consultant, you are going to want to employ a plan from day one to create it happen.

If you would like to begin or reboot your career as an independent consultant, following is a detail by detail strategy to be certain that you're paid well.

1. Pick your specialty

There are a whole lot of people now selling knowledge on the internet on subjects that they do not actually know much about. If you would like to be successful freelancer consultant, you want to decide on a niche where you've got real expertise.

Because you've got an interest in marketing does not mean that you're equipped to turn into successful marketing and advertising adviser. You ought to choose the opportunity to develop extensive knowledge on the subject. Nevertheless, that you never require a ba in marketing to accomplish it. There are a great deal of e-courses and programs out there there to assist you to expand your skill set.

Now inside: under-30

Instead, you may also choose a niche in which you are already considered a professional owing to every entire day occupation.

2. Set your platform up

Next, you will need to set up your own platform to attract customers to your organization. Ordinarily, this really is an internet site. Setting up this is in fact one of many easy parts—determine how to create a site tutorial. What if your internet site comprise? At minimum, you are going to want to have an explanation of one's qualifications, services and also a few reviews to back up you.

Additionally, freelance marketplaces are a fantastic spot to prepare your profile and let customers find you. All these market places frequently possess the bad rap because of being mills where managers get paid ridiculously lower prices but if you are not the renowned neil patel (who accounts charging $5,000 an hour for consulting), " I wouldn't rely just in your own internet site to acquire outcomes.

"free-lancers desire more market places to make leverage and increase earnings," says jeff tennery, ceo of moonlighting, amobile, note-taking program that joins people appearing to operate and make better money with people prepared to employ through its own platform along with dozens of networking spouses. "the more places that salespeople are available, the more customers they are able to procure, increasing interest and high rates. Moonlighting has become accessible more than 150 news outlets just like the chicago tribune, la times and usa today, and is being piled onto 100,000+ verizon mobile apparatus nationally giving anglers more chances to function and much more selection of better paid gigs."

3. Select your speeds

As soon as you have your platform setup, you ought to pick your rates. You might or might not need to print them in your own internet site. Keeping them confidential can provide you the choice to correct them to get certain customers whenever necessary.

Just how much should you charge? That really is the biggest variable that determines how fast you are able to get well-paid. Establish your rates too low, and you will probably spend quite a while busying yourself with job which really doesn't cover nicely.

To get an idea, kennedy information failed a survey of consulting fees to get somebody small direction or it consulting business. They bill $294 each hour normally. In contrast, a different entry adviser charges typically $175 hourly.

To control increased consulting prices, moonlighting ceo, jeff tennery, says you must treat your outsourcing such as the legit firm that it's and put money into promotion using various channels so you're able to generate more attention than it is possible to meet, and also be far selective in the projects that you take in,"that may add price, or general contentment from the undertaking."

4. Start media

The ideal place to start is with your existing personal and professional system. Who would you know just who could send customers your own way? Send emails out to friends and family, loved ones, and former job customers allowing them to know you are available for business and searching for referrals.

Then you have to begin media on the web. Subscribe for social network associated with your industry and participate with people. Establish pro interpersonal networking accounts (notably linked-in and twitter). Start engaging and following together with different professionals that may possibly send referrals your way.

Networking is a continuing procedure you simply can't afford upon. If you would like to turn into highly paid freelance adviser, you cannot let your existing workforce down you. Network always which means you are always watching for better, higher paying customers.

5. Learn how to say no

Certainly one of the greatest fears people have to become a freelancer would be the possibility of never having enough job. Finding customers is straightforward if your speed is very competitive but fulfilling your own hours together with low-paying customers won't ever let your business enterprise scale. This is exactly why you must learn how to say no.

Potential customers will request discount rates. But toe a challenging line along with your rates that are published. Make certain any extra consultations you're all paid off. Your timing isn't entirely free.

If you end up getting overly busy for brand fresh endeavors, it is the right time to increase your rates. Try so frequently in the event that you'd like to actually generate income as an independent consultant.

# 10 essential tools every freelance business needs

## 1. Online collaboration applications

Employed as a freelancer generally means you are cooperating with the others on projects. You want a simple method to speak with your relatives and customers without clogging up your email in box. Use on the web collaboration applications to convey, share and upload documents, delegate tasks and also maintain upon a job's advancement in realtime. Some favorite ones to test are trello, asana, redbooth and podio.

## 2. A bookkeeping method

Use a bookkeeping program to monitor sales and expenses, bill clients, cover employees (when you've got these) and also make your life a great deal easier, specially come tax season. Some favorite bookkeeping tools it is possible to take to are zoho, wave, quickbooks and freshbooks.

## 3. A time monitoring tool

As an expert, you need to be see-through, and liable for, the more billable time you spend money on customers' projects. However, keeping tabs on hours after working on various projects may be nuisance. The best way to go would be to work with a time tracking tool to eliminate the guesswork and also help you save some time. With one click, then you have to keep an eye on the time on activities and send the leads to your clientele. This helps you track your time and effort management competencies, which will be able to assist you to improve your own productivity. Sometime tracking tools to have a look at are slimtimer, toggl along with rescuetime.

## 4. Cloud-based file storage

Employing storage to organize work and discuss with your mates and customers is a excellent idea. It generates your device simpler, provides you with the simplicity of obtaining your files from some other apparatus and ensures that you never lose them in the event that you damage or lose your pc. The hottest options are google-drive and dropbox.

### 5. A job management instrument

For many freelancers, keeping upward on an everyday workload necessitates more than only a todo list. You want a complex task management tool to find the best picture of and enhance your own workload. Wunderlist includes all of the reminder and list skills you can want to maintain on all of your endeavors every afternoon. Google tasks is just another fantastic option which lets you show mails into tasksand sync them along with your own google calendar.

### 6. A movie messaging and chat service

Facetoface meetings stay the finest method to make a comment about prospects and speak with all customers, but you probably do not have to have those if you freelancer on the web. That which you usually want is video conferencing. Utilize video conferencing applications with mobile choices, chat, along with additional exceptional features to really interact to customers. Several popular choices include now skype, rounds, meetingburner, blue-jeans and jabbster.

### 7. A record signing tool

Signing specific contracts and non-disclosure arrangements is a frequent undertaking for salespeople. But print out a record, signing up, scan it and hammering back it requires a good deal of time. Benefit from record signing programs to conserve some time and turn the whole lot in to an entirely digital endeavor. A few options to consider would be pandadoc, echosign and docusign.

### 8. An email management application

Being a freelancer frequently signifies having dozens or hundreds of e mails to manage daily. Cleaning your inbox out can be awkward, if you don't take advantage of an in box management tool. The application may assist you to auto-unsubscribe from unnecessary mails and drive your inbox out clutter fast. It is going to even accommodate to your own special preferences when cleaning your in box, offering filter solutions tailored to suit your own needs. Two amazing options are mailstrom and sanebox.

### 9. A customer database application

The more customers you have, that the harder it would be to maintain your freelancer services personal. Make use of a user database tool such as falcon or even rapportive and you're able to cause advanced level touch profiles directly in your email address or on societal networking. And even in the event that you never have plenty of customers, using these tools to record your prospects can assist you to remember the tiny details that matter the best way to acquire the project.

10. A job suggestion instrument

Creating job tips is just one of the absolute most essential activities for an independent firm to grow and flourish. However, doing them takes a great deal of practice and time. Make use of a job suggestion tool and you're able to slice down the task to moments, creating amazing suggestions with the aid of pre-built landing and templates pages. Several options to think about are bidsketch and proposable.

# 5 gear every freelancer ought to know about

Freelancing is a great livelihood choice today that remote work is now hot and you'll be able to earn a excellent living without leaving home. Whether you are a freelance writer or even a business adviser, all candidates have any small business challenges in keeping, such as optimizing invoicing, coordinating their tasks, scheduling client tasks, and so on. With the appropriate tools, every one of these issues becomes a cinch to address.

Listed below are just five components each freelancer must look into:

1. Invoicing

Invoicing is a underrated tool which creates a big difference. Getting invoices paid promptly with nominal prices will be actually a constant struggle for builders that are susceptible to their customers' budgets and schedules. The easier you'll create this particular process, the quicker you are going to receive money off.

There are a great deal of invoicing program options around, however, a well liked for freelancers will be freshbooks. This cloud bookkeeping applications lets you create professional statements based on templates, and frequently at no cost. It is possible to even use their additional features for bookkeeping.

2. Notetaking

Due to the nature of your job, you're likely on the move a good deal. There isn't set hoursand you're able to work wherever you desire. An individual could say you are always on the clock since you'll work inbetween professional duties whenever you have time. Something to take notes whenever inspiration strikes will probably be invaluable for work.

Evernote is one of the most popular of note taking tools. It's a program that is based on cloud-storage to maintain your filesnotes, receipts, and documents attainable in any way times. You're able to use checklists and labels to remain organized. You might even shoot photos of essential memos or reminders for those who require, coordinating them in accordance with their importance.

3. Shareable calendars

When you have to stick to a single page together with your clientele or alternative collaborators each day, a calendar that is readily shared between most of collaborators is valuable to your own operations. It's going to provide you with the flexibility to schedule appointments with no digital helper. This is very helpful for salespeople at a consulting capacity or perhaps a very similar industry.

Many distant workers use google calendar, that really is an easy shareable tool for people to make use of. But, you may decide to try calendly. It's basically a digital helper which lets you join to google calendars to produce appointments and stay organized together with your clientele. You may invite one to see your availability and program so.

4. Editable document storage

Something which allows you to save and share files on the cloud can be valuable to many freelancers. It is the the ideal method to join and socialize with customers and associates. It's particularly beneficial when you get a handson client who desires to understand your progress and produce their edits or notes on the way.

Google-drive is the hottest and reliable tool of its own kind. It comprises spread sheets, documents, photos, and more which may be shared and edited. With your consent, customers and collaborators will create comments or edit your own content and build an even far more holistic outlook on a job. Best yet, the majority of us have a google account, making usage of google-drive simple sufficient reason for a diminished learning curve.

5. Internet site and program blockers

Many salespeople report their greatest distractions would be the countless programs and internet sites they prefer to go to usually. Social internet sites, games, video loading websites, shopping programs, and much more may be a big diversion once you've got a looming deadline and also little motivation to finish work.

Look in to programs which can obstruct your ability to get into all these anti-productivity programs. Selfcontrol is a helpful program downloaded on the world wide web that could block any internet sites or programs in your own computer that function as a diversion. Use it once you feel unmotivated to eradicate all temptation—you will be amazed how fast you get right back on the right track!

# 5 instrument places for scaling your freelancer business to a full consultancy

More firms are outsourcing their tasks to qualified freelance professionals before, but when you'd like to scale your freelancer business to some complete consultancy (in digital promotion or differently), you the demand that the infrastructure and tools to deal with a bigger client loading.

Listed below are just five goals together with required tools to assist do precisely that.

# FREELANCE CONSULTING: PROVIDE SERVICES TO HIGH TICKET CUSTOMERS. BUILD AND GROW YOUR OWN GIG EMPIRE.

1. Tools for developing the small business

While there's absolutely requirement for outsourced job, it's rather challenging for freelancer professionals to understand the best places to locate the proper jobs.

There are many marketplaces to choose from, targeted at salespeople in all businesses from writing and website site design, to programming, audio/video job, and much more. Options range from the following...

- Unomy: built as being a b2b coding instrument, this specific browser-extension will be able to assist you to construct a listing of targeted potential businesses. The platform enables you filter organizations according to geographical location, size, industry, financing, and much more.
- Upwork: this really is an global selection of accountants in many of businesses. As a freelancer, then you may produce a profile that functions like a portfolio of forms, then find job listings to bidding on. Hourly work requires candidates to put in a program that monitors screen shots and keystrokes.
- Sumome: sumome's package of list-building tools allow you to turn any page in to an conversion funnel. If you have an internet site (so everybody else), then sumome is really a nobrainer for turning blog traffic in to business leads.
- Fiverr: somewhat different from the conventional freelancer market, this site enables salespeople to make a oneoff task they truly are ready to complete for 5, together with extras to get extra money. Guidelines may also be a choice, therefore even though the bottom actions begin at $5, then getting speeds can be a lot greater.

2. Maintain decent track of jobs and financing

Free-lancers currently wear several hats over the span of daily, frequently tackling all parts of the company. To conserve some time, as well as possibly a lot of sanity too, it is really a fantastic idea to put money into work flow management software.

- Workflowmax: this cloud-based platform manages several elements of conducting the business all in 1 platform. It has quotes, job costing, time sheets, invoices, and job administration. Employing a job management system conserves time as you never need to modify from stage to platform to take care of tasks, time tracking, and invoicing/billing. It works nicely for unmarried teams and workers. Becoming cloud-based, it might be accessed anywhere there is an online connection, which makes it simple for people that work onthego.

- Because : still another timetracking and invoicing program, since supports over 100 states and taxation systems, heavensent for salespeople who have to learn how to control their own financing and taxation obligations. The program supports integration using thirdparty solutions such as quickbooks, base-camp and pay pal, reducing the effort required to control bills, tasks and time lines.

3. Collaborate wisely

Working from home does not need to be isolating. There will undoubtedly be instances within the course of jobs whenever you will have to collaborate with other folks. As a result of this accessible resources, space is perhaps not an problem.

- Skype for industry works wonders whenever you require basic tele conferencing. Additionally, it enables video or voice conversation, with the selection to talk about displays. Add ons ensure it is straightforward to record the requirements for inspection after. The complimentary skype variant ought to be capable of easy chats, video and voice calls.

Clickmeeting is a perfect solution for remote on the web training, specially for one-to-many discussions. This really is a superb option for companies that have to prepare the freelancers that they hire. But in addition, it functions for salespeople that wish to outsource a few of their daily small business activities to other salespeople.

4. Automate tasks

# FREELANCE CONSULTING: PROVIDE SERVICES TO HIGH TICKET CUSTOMERS. BUILD AND GROW YOUR OWN GIG EMPIRE.

Automation helps maintain the small business running easily while focusing your efforts on more essential tasks. Business regularly check freelance programmers and it professionals in managing programs such as enterprise resource planning (erp) and customer relationship management (crm) solutions.

Automating the patching, upgrading and upgrading procedure for all these enterprise software with an instrument such as panaya will guarantee that advisers and also the it department is going to have additional hours for you to wait core tasks as opposed to dull tasks.

- Social networking: a b2b social media marketing management platform, oktopost enables entrepreneurs and salespeople automate and assess the achievements of their societal campaigns. As soon as it isn't always such a fantastic strategy to completely conduct societal networking stations on auto pilot, oktopost provides a method to program and queue content much beforehand. Make sure you register a couple of minutes daily to take part in live discussions.

- Storage: tools such as drop-box, one drive along with box supply a way to store records on the web. Better still, these programs enable freelancers to sync with certain folders and files, allowing easy cooperation with customers. Professional variations have versioning support, so therefore that you are able to keep tabs on files because they change.
- Client service: salespeople that regularly connect to clients and desire a easy tool for managing interactions using endusers. An customer support solution platform such as zendesk may automate service tickets, generate a knowledgebase, and also manage faqs.

5. Watch for tendencies

More companies are ongoing to start looking for methods to outsource activities to consultants and freelancers. Sexy businesses for advisers include: ecofriendly, smallbusiness expertise, and it security. It isn't just tiny organizations which are trying to outsource work.

Even larger ventures are beginning to count on freelance professionals and advisers to find work done. We are able to expect that the market place to become more info, as well as different facets of business.

- Google trends can be actually a superb spot to keep monitoring of trending issues. As the search parameters are quite limited, you may keep tabs business-specific trends or view performance with the years to get key words.
- Free-lancing books like the freelancer and electronic advertising and marketing blogs similar to that 1 right here may also be a wonderful resource for tracking trends and understanding what's going on out your distinct sphere.

# Chapter six: Type of customers freelancer should avoid

## 4 kinds of freelance customers you need to avoid at all costs

Once you have awakened the 9to5, your timing is a type of money, and also you need to utilize it sensibly. Therefore as you are attempting to conclude with a challenging client or focusing on re-do after re-do for someone you cannot seem to please, then you are wasting time you might possibly be spending getting money from different projects.

To remain effective and struggle freelance-related frustration, stay away of these subsequent four kinds of customers when selecting your second gig.

1. The "i don't really understand what I am on the lookout to get"

No matter how great your job is, in the event the customer does not understand exactly what she wants (or can, however, it is perhaps not realistic), you'll either wind up feeling frustrated.

Thus, before choosing a freelancer mission, have a dialog with your customer where you talk specifically about her targets. Share her ultimate fantasies, in addition to a few more realistic targets. What exactly does she need done within the upcoming week? Think about the next year? All these ought to be concrete dreams which you may focus. Additionally, learn just how she measures success: a "increase in traffic" can mean something different for you than it's to her, therefore be certain that you set quantifiable particulars.

As an additional notice, as soon as you've heard exactly what she expects to do, be certain you truly feel just like it's possible to deliver. As an instance, if your heart skill is writing, there isn't any doubt in denying a job that is really focused more about interpersonal networking. The customer will appreciate the honesty, and could contact you in case your writing job appears later on. But if you attempt to pretend it and wind up badly under-delivering, your reputation endures.

## 2. The houdini

That really is actually the customer who's slow to answer mails and occasionally appears to just evaporate entirely, dismissing your voicemails and followup mails (even the people marked"urgent!"). Even though this might not look like a enormous bargain, a client who wishes to lose the surface of this earth can delay your advancement and also cause issues in regards to crucial transactions—such as being paidoff.

By way of example, I had been thrilled to property a high-paying freelance occupation by an entrepreneur, however less thrilled after I waited for days ahead to find a solution to a brief question. I was less pleased when I placed in lots of hours of effort just to discover my paycheck had not come along with that your customer had been no where available.

That really is a trickier issue to grab from the beginning, however, your initial two or three interactions with an customer can supply some insight to the way he works. When he chooses a week to reply to an instant e mail about the facts of the mission or your own contract, then he will most likely not have enough time to provide timely responses. Oryou know, cover you.

## 3. The use less barterer

Swapping services can be a fantastic way to associate with a fresh client, specially one that wants assistance but might not need enough money to cover your commission. However, before investing in, make certain that you're both profiting from the offer.

For instance, if you are composing e-mail newsletters to get a salon as a swap for free hair cuts, it might be a reasonable swap. You are always going to want hair cuts, right? However if you are being offered free base ball tickets for the custom logo and you also despise sports, then you most likely shouldn't accept that the transaction. This sort of barter system just works if you should be saving cash on some thing that you'd need to purchase anyway, so ask for payment in cash or turndown the undertaking.

## FREELANCE CONSULTING: PROVIDE SERVICES TO HIGH TICKET CUSTOMERS. BUILD AND GROW YOUR OWN GIG EMPIRE.

Before beginning, determine just how you'll determine payment. Is it hourly? Per job? Never merely say,"oh, we will figure out it by the ending." decide on a regular for payment beforehand and then stay to it. And do make certain your transaction is rational. A vest to get a newsletter swap is reasonable. A hair cut to fully update the whole company site? Not too much.

4. The rate dater

Here really is actually the customer with really gone through most, many salespeople before landing. I knowi understand: much enjoy chasing the badboy or the partygirl, it's easy to feel as if you're able to be the only one to improve a consumer, even though the others until you've neglected.

I did, also: I took to a brand new gig, and so was convinced that I was able to send your site articles that this client wanted. Though he'd cautioned me he'd experienced many of freelance authors in years past I was not concerned. Ends up, I have to have beeni wound up wasting some time with a lot of re writes, without a true guidance concerning what the prior articles were lacking. It became evident that client could never be very happy.

Before signing onto utilize some body, learn for their previous experience with other professionals in the own industry. Ask the possible client about her or his job together with previous free-lancers and, even if you're able to, speak with several the salespeople you to ultimately acquire their sides of this narrative. You may explain that you may love to acquire some insight to what worked and what did not so you are able to organize your approach effortlessly.

In case he is not comfortable placing you connected his old flames, atleast strive to do just a bit of research on these. In case the previous workers are typical respectable professionals with strong backgrounds, then the issue might well not have now been with all the salespeople in any way, but together with all the customer. But whether or not it's apparent that the previous concerns were as a result of this freelancers' workforce, that is different.

While some fantastic occupation depends on a work place which lets you become prosperous, it will become particularly crucial once you are going at it independently like a freelancer. Do not sell yourself short or put yourself up for failure by either dealing with customers that are finicky, maybe not keen to cover or even hard to accomplish. Alternatively, forget the frustration and holdout to customers with realistic objectives and also open lines of communication.

# 7 different types of bad customers every newbie freelancer should know

Being your supervisor is a whole great deal simpler nowadays. When you possess a certain skill or ability, then it is simple to monetize it to make money. Being a freelancer permits one to roll into the considerable quantity of money from the convenience of one's house. Now, salespeople are a parallel job which generates just as much money as fulltime workers earn out of a workplace.

In addition, a profession in outsourcing permits one to devote your spare time for earning profits without being liable to anybody. You may earn a livelihood in outsourcing even once you're employed as a fulltime professional. Afterall, who heads cashing in certain additional money? Additionally, there are fulltime employees who've been blessed enough to allow it to be a very thriving livelihood.

Exactly like any other business, the first phase to an effective outsourcing company is customer retention. But, it's really a bit tricky to catch customers like a freelancer compared to a traditional small business.

Contrary to a planetary facility, your outsourcing company includes virtual contact points that keep the customers abreast about the real you. Therefore they are inclined to think before making a bargain with you.

Even once you have some customers in your pocket, another step is always to maintain them pleased with your products and services. This takes a fantastic comprehension of one's niche and the kinds of customers you're likely to take care of. Nonetheless, it's the debatable customers who have the majority of your time and effort whenever you begin like a freelancer.

Expand to find the table of contents

# FREELANCE CONSULTING: PROVIDE SERVICES TO HIGH TICKET CUSTOMERS. BUILD AND GROW YOUR OWN GIG EMPIRE.

What defines a problematic client?

It's normal to find a few debatable customers once you start off. Nevertheless, you need to keep in mind that timing is the largest barrier in bringing through the outsourcing job and addressing the undesirable clients is 1 of the ways that you waste this precious resource.

A lousy customer is somebody who can be oblivious of the industry or gets the right facts of a job, along with the worse he could be someone who chooses to cover the amount of money after conclusion of his job.

Working with poor customers demands some urge and intellect. However, most importantly, it needs a few experience. Depending on experiences among these folks, we provide here several shared kinds of bad customers and the way it is possible to handle them. They are:

1. Never satisfied

Some clients are just never pleased however hard you try. They are going to consistently request alterations or re-designs that reveal too little admiration for the own time.

In case a customer is advertising asking one to reevaluate work even if you're convinced it is up to level, now is the time for you to part ways. Do not become influenced by the idea of losing a few dollars as you may lose more money in the shape of wasted moment.

Have a look at the individual element. You want to be certain in the event the customer is treating you prefer a machine along with even a servant? Freelancing isn't a straightforward job and, hence, the customers need to honor your time just as far because they can do someone who plays with a 9 to 5 job.

If you end up pressured to haggle with a client to get a minimal amount or even to do tasks not mentioned from the arrangement, you almost certainly need these customers.

But if they do not pay heed your own reasons and also don't quit endangering youpersonally, you need to make an effort to finish their projects as fast as you possibly can and bow out. Make certain that you receive money until you leave, though.

2. The mr. Perfectionists

Such a customer is different to hinder every thing. As soon as it's okay if a buyer covers his job and assesses it for correction, then it's maybe not reasonable to request adjustments marketing.

Nearly all perfectionists have been prone to arguing every final thing with the freelancer, even while it's actually a trivial grammatical mistake or grammatical mistakes with zero bearing on the grade of the task done.

The only way you can handle perfectionist customers is by simply complying with their guidelines. Avoid the desire to put in your inputs since they'll sooner or later deny them and all of your efforts will come in vain.

3, ignorant

Nothing is as annoying as addressing an unlearned customer who's unaware of their or her own business enterprise. This strain of clients isn't conscious of the styles of the marketplace and so lacks the master plan for communication with a freelancer.

The most peculiar thing about this type of customers is they have a tendency to contend with you over matters they don't really possess some hint and you also don't have any option except to condone their negative behaviour.

Giving clear directions or guidelines appears close to impossible in their mind. The majority of the full time rookie salespeople would become frustrated to the idea of losing his or her mind.

Most times it's all about asks for changes within the past second. Only when you're just about to finish a job, they educate one to own it done another way around. Seasoned candidates, nevertheless, would chalk this up to have, given they take the task with no details at the first.

# FREELANCE CONSULTING: PROVIDE SERVICES TO HIGH TICKET CUSTOMERS. BUILD AND GROW YOUR OWN GIG EMPIRE.

The only way to prevent such customers wasting your time and effort, energy and reassurance is always to make certain that you receive all the directions ahead. Never begin working straight off; request schedule a consultation, a gathering, or find the important points and details at a email. This would demand a little bit of handson experience whilst the specific details some times can't be fathomed.

The fantastic news isthat every evil experience can also be a learning experience, therefore learn from the past and apply it to prospective customers and endeavors.

## 4. Indecisive

Addressing an indecisive customer is one among the hardest experiences that you might get like a freelancer. Such customers have a tendency to stay changing their mind in regards to the prognosis of these undertaking. Taking endeavors in various instructions is the favourite pastime. You're going to be spending energy, time, and skill drafts and suggestion which is going to soon be of no usage at the ending of your afternoon.

Again the only way to take care of these customers is to receive the important points, directions and plans directly at first prior to starting work. When it's impossible, you want to determine whether you're able to require damages for the drafts, that will be just fair. Stand your rights up within certain constraints.

## 5. A form of customers who never agree

Your customer does not need to function as a single individual and you also might be employers who'd dictate you that a project. Should they're professional, then they'll assign you the job following approval of their top honcho of this undertaking. Such classes may be joy to work together, since they have been experienced and always available for any questions that you might have.

Alternatively, if they often have regular arguments concerning the endeavors, then a job is the most likely aborted at the midst. There's also a chance they request alterations over and over.

Amidst such a circumstance, you want to carefully confer with this client to keep on with the undertaking and straight back with your own payment.

6. Awol

There are a lot of laid back men and women that are unlikely to call you back or answer that a text. Bear in mind, in the modern world of complex technology; there needs to not be any excuse to keep incommunicado unless you're out for a secondary or stranded on a desert island.

For these customers, you want to send a couple e mails to verify details as an evaluation at the start of your job and find out just how long they choose to answer. When it's significantly more than the usual week, then you should prepare for long waits in receiving the answers or work out how exactly to slip him away.

7. Non committal

Afterward you will find customers who want to evaluate your expert expertise by simply requesting your qualifications. They won't even bother providing you with a project at substantially lesser speed.

There's nothing incorrect when a customer really wants to be aware of the expert foundation of a freelancer, but make sure you recognize the warning flag. The greatest of these will be again enough full time wastage.

You may be forced to undergo infinite suggestions, consultations and price discussions, yet the occupation does not suffice for quite a while.

## How to identify and prevent terrible customers being a freelancer

Bad customers are anyplace.

Like a freelancer at the specialist jungle, it's really a matter of success to comprehend awful clients until you waste your time and income.

# FREELANCE CONSULTING: PROVIDE SERVICES TO HIGH TICKET CUSTOMERS. BUILD AND GROW YOUR OWN GIG EMPIRE.

With restricted legal ability and financial means, you're in the base of the expert food series. Your greatest strategy can be to determine abusive customers prior to later.

Discussing freelancers who travelled through debilitating pro adventures, we assembled a comprehensive collection of red flags which will help you build into a 6th sense.

Truth will be made on the customer side, naturally. Perhaps not most them are knowledgeable about salespeople. Use your decision in regards to employing cut throats techniques, some times a quick conversation goes a very long way.

Ahead of the job begins (the ideal interval)

The following warning flags will habitually be increased very soon. Using these in your mind, you ought to really be equipped to filter bad customers before you work one minute.

They do not inquire on your charge

First thing, do not let your cost turned into a taboo. When a client provides you tasks before knowing just how much it will cost, they probably have not jammed youpersonally, should they really have a budget in any way. A cost/benefit investigation is pretty hard with no fee element. They'll act surprised once you send them a statement and can attempt to negotiate down you once the project is finished.

Their short term is quite obscure

This customer has not completed its homeworks, and also the pressure will be in your own shoulders. He's got quite a vague and delusional idea by what he needs, and the majority of that time period based on results obtained by different businesses.

It'll be very debilitating to find out exactly what they will have in your mind. As it isn't part of a reliable plan, the master plan will probably change a number of period at a very inconsistent way. They aren't gonna-be eager to cover and can set the blame for you for not establishing what they did not understand they wanted exactly the very first moment.

They seem cluttered

In case you cannot actually get a clear response within reasonable waits before a project starts, only imagine what it is going to be like within a crunch period together with competitive milestones.

If multiple men and women are concerned, it will get somewhat harder, as main information is going to likely be lost in translation.

If the program affects several times, at a really polar fashion, before you start working, expect vision changes at the center of this undertaking.

They attempt to cut your speed radically

You're a micro business, behave like it. As soon as it's ok to lower your fee in the event that you observe strict rules, agreeing with some ridiculously low cost wont do you some good. Taking care of this undertaking will probably be bothersome, your patience is likely to soon be lower and also the general level of work may possibly reduce.

Stay away out of them. They do not respect that your job.

They discuss providing you vulnerability

Do not walk off. Run a way.

They need things for free

The only complimentary things that you need to devote is your portfolio. It needs to be sufficient to allow them to observe the standard of one's output and find out whenever they desire similar outcomes.

Do not let them place the dangers of their job in your own shoulders with you work free of charge and just pay if it's what they had in your mind. They frequently have several freelancers focus with suggestions - that really isn't a competition, you deserve to receive money.

# FREELANCE CONSULTING: PROVIDE SERVICES TO HIGH TICKET CUSTOMERS. BUILD AND GROW YOUR OWN GIG EMPIRE.

"i have been through lots of free-lancers before I found."

The majority of times you are able to interpret that to "other agendas such as you did not accept my violent conditions".

Bear in mind the e card that stated "the only continuous in all of your failed relationships is that you." if you are able to keep in touch with some other salespeople who understand client, simply to ensure that your intuition is ideal. Unless you're far above average (the alpha), the issue is just about your customer.

They wish to begin now (or even yesterday)

No contract, no vision, no. Instructions, no specs, no no agreement.

That is not being lean, so this really is being reckless. It is going to back-fire quickly, as any salespeople with somewhat of experience can tell (debilitating memories, huh?).

Always search for the worst and most also make sure each one the core questions have been answered before you get started workingout. Take to needing at the very least a written agreement (it can possibly be a email or even a contract), it's not a powerful legal ground, however it's much better than nothing.

Through the job (you have been baited)

Some customers are experts at the artwork of deception and figure out how to earn their job look very exciting at the beginning. They may even be conscious of the earlier cited warning flags and force you to believe they're a specie of amazing customers. If you happen across someone of these warning flags, then simply understand that it had been just camouflage.

They always change the deadlines and prerequisites

If you're dealing with multiple customers every day, this is likely to soon be nightmare. Plan a very shaky program your priorities will likely be assessed immediately, you are going to understand it deadline 4 hours before departing for holiday season.

The acceptance arrangement is complicated

If the manager must get it approved by producer who must make it approved by the art director that needs to make it approved by the ceo who must make it approved by his spouse, rest assured you're wind up receiving curve balls.

They return on things they consented on awhile ago

A symptom of this prior red flag. Your job experienced the entire approval procedure, it had been authenticated by each and every decisionmaker on the customer side. Yet, a couple of weeks afterwards, somebody at the control series shifted his brain and you'll certainly be asked to re do every thing.

They deny upfront obligations

Section of working is sharing risk. Receiving an upfront payment (15-50 percent, usually) is really a fantastic indication of a healthful method of trading. It compels every one to be cooperative, and also you wont fear they pull on out the plug of the gloomy.

As a general principle, do not work too much with no paid, bill early and bill regularly.

They believe what's a little repair

"could you make our site available on mobile telephone for our presentation to morrow ?"

The inherent complexity of your job must be known, at least partially. It's the obligation to educate them concerning exactly what these minor modifications signal. The foolish concessions tend to be asked by customers with very lower expertise on your domain of activity.

Things frequently seem easy after you don't know.

They think they understand more than you do

Confident customers that have simply no idea what they are doing certainly are an incredibly dangerous specie. Their gut atmosphere will over rule several years of expertise. They have been completely inconsistent and certainly will shamelessly violate the rules of one's livelihood repeatedly. These customers hire you for the expertise yet do not recognize it. Oh incidentally, in the long run, after a few hours of futile micro management, they'll blame you for hearing them.

Their job environment is exceptionally governmental

You abandoned the corporate world to become far out of politics, have not you? If you're not a freelancer psychologist, then it ought to be described as a red flag if a customer keeps draining his soul about his supervisor and coworkers. A conflict of vision and worth is happening in the client organization, and also you may possibly face the results sooner or later. Be cautious.

How to proceed?

Listed below are a couple of tips which may help you take care of demanding customers.

- Speak with these, some times they simply do not find out about your dissatisfaction and also a swift discussion can correct plenty of issues in the future.
- Do not collect anger, so it is going to create any possible conversation filled with emotions.
- Stay professional, so that you never want to mess up your reputation.
- Be adaptive, business is insanity, your customers probably have alot in the shoulders too.
- Suggest solutions, nobody likes a whiner.

# Chapter seven: Common mistakes a freelancer must avoid at all cost

## 7 errors salespeople ought to prevent

Not many freelancers are selfemployed from the beginning. Usually self-employment is completed by routine usage. Employed as a freelancer regularly presents several disadvantages and may pose unanticipated challenges. As soon as it's normal to make mistakes, there are a few which is readily avoided. Here we've put together a set of mistakes which salespeople should avoid under most conditions.

1. Missed deadlines

Your value for a freelancer is depending on the premium quality of work, that you simply send in mutually agreed obligations. Consistently meeting deadlines can allow you to build a favorable standing—along with your own reputation is whatever that you need. By comparison, missing deadlines causes enormous issues for you personally and certainly will very quickly sour a client relationship.

To be sure you get jobs done punctually, estimate how long you will need for each job and give yourself just a little additional time. Unexpected delays and complications can always occur. Having job milestones is just another very helpful way to be certain that a job is done by the deadline. In the event you forget a deadline, your clients will just take their business else where. So: punctuality is vital.

2. Being true to yourself

Specially at the start, free-lancers are worried to reel in as many projects as you possibly can as a way to obtain experience. This attitude is usually accurate. But, it isn't necessarily in your interest to accept every deal. In depth research before accepting a deal is vital. Determine by which business the consumer is busy and if this suits your expertise. Speak to some other salespeople, that have worked to your customer and choose whether you're exactly the ideal man for the occupation. For those who have doubts regarding the job from the start, the outcome will not be that excellent.

## 3. Confusing company with joy

Though you can utilize a more relaxed tone together with your web visitors as a freelancer, then you should however keep a certain amount of professionalism. Ofcourse you can conduct business with buddies or have customers that become friendsnevertheless, it's vital that you get a differentiation between both of these worlds. By applying a specific expert manner of business tasks, you may produce a very clear differentiation between both of these worlds.

## 4. Getting mad with a customer

It may occur that you just get exasperated with an individual, sometimes justly therefore. But do not make the error of becoming mad with the customer and also writing a rude email or increasing your voice. Reign on your anger and dismiss steam everywhere, but not having your customer. This is only going to allow you to seem unprofessional and leaves a poor feeling. Once the preliminary anger has vanished, you should seek out a dialog with your customer at a professional stage, with no emotional consequences, and go over the issue as a way to prevent future misunderstandings.

## 5. Do not suggest follow up jobs

Many salespeople believe it successfully finished endeavor is sufficient to create follow-up jobs. While you successfully completed endeavor can usually result in more gigs, it is better to not assume. A better strategy is to offer your customer with further choices to make money from the services. Be useful and crucial.

## 6. Do not place your eggs all in a single basket

It's a bad idea to own just one or two sources of income for being a freelancer. For any variety of reasons, why it's possible that the customer can't cover you to get a continuous job or you are having difficulty locating work. Whatever the problem may be, it's very important that you've got several sources of revenue and many weeks of economies to make certain you're able to cover most of your own expenses.

7. Dealing with too many jobs

As you are your own boss and decide if and how long you are working, it could be tempting to undertake multiple endeavors to boost your cash flow. But, it will be potential to fall prey to burn out if you undertake a lot of endeavors.

Flexibility is 1 benefit of self-employment. In the event you have to have a step back and then focus with fewer jobs, then you can concentrate on marketing yourself or renovating your own office at home.

# 8 truth free-lancers be you ought to avoid

Whether you are a veteran freelancer or beginning, we've made our fair share of mistakes on the way. Some times that mistake is little and it's really only a hassle for you and the customer. Other occasions, an error might be detrimental by that you simply get rid of a customer or suffer a monetary loss. In any event, acquiring a slide up here and there's not always this awful. Learning out of the blunder is among the very best ways to know.

However, why take that opportunity?

Listed below are just 8 errors which free-lancers should be avoided in any way costs.

1. Unsure what you are worth

That is possibly the principal mistake that freelancers always create—specially if they get in to outsourcing. There is this misconception which they must charge lower rates or offer discounts so as to bring customers. Which could work with just a bit. However, what happens in the event that you begin getting referrals? These new customers are getting to likewise anticipate that speed now you're painting yourself into a corner. On the opposite end of the spectrum, even should you charge a lot of prospective customers might be look else where.

This is what though. Even though clients definitely need to find the best bang for their dollar, they are prepared to pay you everything you are worth—actually marginally higher—in the event that you should be exceptional at what you're doing.

To help determine your value and also place your prices, here is a handful questions which you ought to ask:

· can you really go to school to master your own abilities?

· just how much experience have you got?

· how competitive is the field of expertise?

· exactly what exactly are the others charging on your own industry? (it is possible to utilize pay-scale to think of a few figures.)

· how much can it cost for one to finish a job?

· what's your overhead? (expenses such as rent, power, managing prices)

Answering questions such as this may offer you a far better idea on just how much to bill. Gleam convenient bill rate calculator that will help you determine just how much you really have to really be charging.

Remember. You need your speeds to be competitive, however you must earn an income—that explains the reason why you won't ever under-charge for the services. Furthermore, if you are a jedi master a consumer isn't likely to worry about paying you longer than simply freelancers that are not as competent. Know your values and also establish the suitable speed which is most appropriate for you personally.

2. Taking too much work

Here is another error that free-lancers encounter in to. It's tempting to undertake every occupation whenever you are beginning. Heck. You carry on to defend myself against job since you are concerned that there might be a period as soon as your workload will get damaged.

# FREELANCE CONSULTING: PROVIDE SERVICES TO HIGH TICKET CUSTOMERS. BUILD AND GROW YOUR OWN GIG EMPIRE.

The issue with this is that you are able to just do as much work daily before you begin delivering workout. More to the point, you run in the probability to growing burn out if you are only working on endeavors 24/7.

Know your limitations how much operate it's possible for you to deal with. Like a writer, I am aware that I cannot do a lot more than 4 or 3 extended articles every day. When your client requests a post arrangement I may possibly need to politely decline the sequence easily curently have articles inside the offing. Ori could require the client whether they are able to wait a couple weeks. It isn't necessarily fun turning a project, however your client should honor your honesty. They'd prefer to have you give them the entire attention. Sometimes that implies you've got to find another person. However, there've been instances once your customer will wait patiently until i've got the opportunity to focus with a job for them.

3. Deficiency of communication

In case you have been engaged in almost any type of connection than you know exactly how important communication is. The same goes between a freelancer and also a customer. Frequent communication may prevent errors and flaws in either the advancement of a job or becoming paid when done.

Before choosing a job, be aware the scope of this job, just how much the job will probably cost, and also just how to get intouch with the customer. Be certain the client has explained exactly what they want to find so when it is anticipated to become finished. Despite you've begun the job, give your client frequent upgrades. When there is some concerns or flaws, do not be afraid to make the client understand. They can find a bit frustrated, however it's far better than turning within a job which is beyond the deadline with no client knowing.

In short, keep the traces of communication open between you and your customer. It's only a little step up establishing a strong connection with you along with your consumer.

4. Holding the incorrect gig

Again, there is always an exaggeration to continue as many tasks as you possibly can. Nonetheless, you could well not be a fantastic fit for several tasks. Maybe the task simply will not interest you. And, that is completely okay. If you would rather creating and submitting articles on healthy living, you might fear choosing projects that are devoted to finance.

There is also scenarios in which you are not seasoned for a job. You could have heard the principles of designing a site, however you aren't a specialist nonetheless. Nonetheless, make use of the amount of money. Thus, you accept work which you aren't capable to accomplish. That is not fair for you or your customer.

We got to freelancer since we want to bust from this 9to5 grind. It's okay to deny a project that individuals do not enjoy because we find it boring or do not have the skill degree.

5. Scrambling to meet with a deadline

Merely as you've got flexibility does not indicate you could ignore deadlines. If you would like to have a week away and move on holiday, then it is possible to. Simply do not freak out when you there exists a deadline awaiting you whenever you buy home. If you would like to carry on more projects than you are able to handle, then do it. Simply do not get frazzled if your customers keep asking you the deadline has not been met.

For whatever reason, it is not rare to get a freelancer to rush into a job so as to contain it done in time. This over-promising and under-performing isn't planning to discuss with your own clients—and it's really definitely going to harm your standing. They expect quality work from you by the deadline that you consented upon.

Again, in case you cannot deal with the workload, there's no necessity to just accept work. In addition, in the event that you fail to finish a mission by a deadline, either due to an unforeseen situation, be fair with the customer.

The best way to prevent any issues though, would be to aim to own the deadline met per day or 2 in progress. This provides you with slightly more flexibility if there is a crisis or whether you should be backed up in your job.

6. Maybe not fixing your freelance career like a small business

Do not kid yourself. After you turned into a freelancer, so you turned into a selfemployed business proprietor. As a company operator, you want to create a business program, set an authorized thing, cover your own taxes, choose the perfect insurance, maintain your books organized, and also ship professional quotes and statements.

Though salespeople and customers agree with a job via a contact correspondence, you can also wish to look at registering up a contract. This will avoid both parties out of bailing on eachother. Smashing magazine includes a list of do's and cann'ts with freelancer contracts.

7. Never waiting for assistance

Just as you are a freelancer does not signify that entirely independently. If you should be overrun or want information you should reach from coworkers or other managers. You might possibly be able to out source a project to a person creative. You might ask a question about a job, paying taxes, or just how to handle your time and effort for being a freelancer. Between societal networking stations, internet sites such as quora, and forums just like the freelance forum, then it's possible to readily reach outside in order to discover a helping hands.

## Avoid these 10 common free-lancing traps to perform a more productive writing business

Do you know such top-ten customs that maintain a freelancer out of taking advantage money whilst remaining trouble? In descending order, here you go:

1. Working with no signed contract

Working with no crystal-clear deal leaves the door available to loopholes, conflicts, delays in charge, no charge and different headaches.

Working with no contract is just one of, maybe even the largest obstacle for freelancers. Be respectful and professional, however get all of the job fees, schedules and terms written down and be certain to know all of the clauses in your arrangement. I talked to a single writer who signed up a contract, did not read the fineprint, also discovered it said her informative article could be outstanding! Still another gave his rights away with no extra charge.

You want a strong contract in order that when extent creep happens—that the client starts wanting to incorporate a growing number of items without additional pay—you still have the contract to refer to say,"that isn't a portion of that which we consented " and after that indicate a fee which could be good for this extra work. With no contract, so it's quite difficult to guard yourself against scope creep. And extent creep surpasses your hourly rate.

2. Not needing a deposit/retainer at the beginning of a small business writing endeavor

In case a company customer is not ready to cough up any money at the onset of a job, it's usually hard to gather by the ending result. When a consumer balks at giving you for a deposit retainer at the start, it is really a waving big, red flag saying,"i really don't trust you" without common confidence there isn't any writer/client romantic relationship.

Adding a deposit or retainer shows to a client you are a skilled and have repayment coverages set up. Chances areyour client will probably honor you as a business person. If prospects yell at paying 30-50percent front, my experience can be that you did not need that client any way—it is really a excellent litmus test that displays out scents. Very good customers pay that with out a blink. They comprehend how free-lancers operate their enterprise and this is needed.

3. Not always marketing your freelance writing solutions

In case an independent writer stalls their marketing campaigns they can readily be swept up in notorious feast-or-famine syndrome. When that occurs, it might have quite a very long time to grab up. The earnings curve for all creative service companies will be just six or eight weeks. That is time in the contact to signing up a deal. Six or eight weeks, or longer, is quite a while to watch for your second cash back. It is vital to get a lot of prospects in various points on your selling procedure.

Editors may take weeks to decide to assign an guide, too. You require a whole lot of lines from the water to guarantee a steady flow of work.

4. Working to the incorrect type of customers

In case you are listening to all of this believing,"contracts? Negotiate? My work stems out of e-lance, or perhaps a material mill, at which they dictate each of the stipulations and cover. I write for earnings discuss ad-click bucks. How can I negotiate a lift or perform "

If those really are the customers, these are the incorrect type of customers. Pay will probably remain low and it is going to never receive any better. You'll always be stuck together with their rockbottom flat speed for articles, or else you will forever able to the ground, pitted against countless different authors, or even waiting mostly in vain to allow your own articles to find enough traffic to enable you to get longer than a dollar.

The huge majority of them situations are not anything lacking writer manipulation. Plus so they won't change. Passively tapping on a platform's dash for missions isn't just how to earning a significant freelancer income.

You need to become a pro active entrepreneurs and proceed outside and identify and also sell far better caliber customers. Or are always going to be needing to work long hours for very little cover. That brings us to...

5. Never requesting a boost

Writers forget to negotiate increases with ongoing customers. I talked to a writer recently who explained she had been writing for a continuing customer for 1-2 decades! And she desired to learn just how exactly to approach them of a raise. Do not allow this to happen!

When you work to get a customer, your value to them rises because you know in their book's their business clients. You eventually become worth more, and also the problem of training a newcomer on that which you realize becomes a lot of hassle. You must find out just how exactly to create chances to readily require and receive increases to your contract. That brings us to...

6. Being fearful to negotiate

For a great deal of authors, once the client sends them a contract, and sometimes maybe merely tells them the terms they need they hear or see that a lot within which makes them more nervous. However they don't really believe they're able to do anything on it, plus so they simply agree.

Negotiating is not complaining, also will not make customers leave—perhaps not excellent ones. The most peculiar thing a potential can do whenever you request improve a contract will be they'll say no more. Then you'll be able to choose whether you would like to choose the gig. But pushing for whatever you feel you deserve in an contract is exactly what professional freelancers perform.

7. Maybe not knowing your rights

You want to know your rights drawing this arrangement, too—and also lots of authors do not. Following that, you understand after you might have retained any confirmation and made more attempting to sell work to additional customers. Usage rights are similar to a dish you are able to slice up asneeded. Plus, usage rights are sometimes a handy discussion tool.

Magazine and several other federal magazines exactly the same task! Entrepreneur magazine simply buys original rights and you'll be able to resell it 3 months after publication in this magazine. As my experience showsthat you would like to keep such rights in the event that it is possible to. They are able to be a goldmine.

On your job instruction, include a move of rights form which is handed on to a client whenever they will have paid. Negotiating and shifting usage rights upon full payment may defuse any payment struggles that might appear.

8. Not intending your company and setting attainable goals

In case an independent author does not possess a plan set up, they risk with their business only occur to them as opposed to calculating a sound path for victory. It is how folks wind up writing for articles mills for a long time—they usually do not possess their eyes onto their own objectives, or an activity program which is due to using a company program.

If your company aims are fuzzy, it's fairly hard to tell if you should be making progress or falling behind. Goals must be realistic and attainable. If your objectives are too hurtful it's simple to become frustrated and neglect. Look at devoting large goals into smaller ones which can be easier to attain.

9. Not understanding just how much it costs you. To maintain operation

Simply pulling out numbers from this atmosphere (imagining) isn't a wonderful business idea. You ought to first make an effort to determine what your competition is charging, and what sort of hosting will be suitable for the enterprise, and also other facets before pulling the trigger. Your basic rates should bear into account your target wages (or draw), overhead and a profit margin (read my article about setting prices. Only change"designer" into"writer" and you're going to be ok.).

There is a popular myth outthere that freelance composing is a nocost firm—right imagine it. Hard disks expire. Monitors go belly up. You may require expert clothing for meetings. As well as also your household includes costs, too—leasing or even a mortgage or car payments or anything you have got. There are also costs! Discover what yours arenow. This can allow you to decide a hourly rate which renders you profit after expenses to keep afloat.

10. Struggling to correctly handle several customers and projects

You may be a talented writer with strong pro se. Or, maybe you are an exemplary writing rain-maker once it involves earnings and final job duties. These are coveted faculties however, perhaps not overly useful in case there is a tough time managing several clients and projects. Juggling a lot of material can get your stomach churn. When that comes to pass, errors soon follow. Customers start whining and also you're running in to the wee hours, on week ends and too frequently with a gloomy time.

Having job management coverages and work flow systems set up are rather crucial whether you would like to maintain your customers contented and maintain your sanity. Joyful customers have a tendency to pay for your bills fast and without complaining. They also may save a little cash on antacids.

# Conclusion

A freelancer operates individually, selling services or work at the hour, day, or occupation usually without the intention to pursue a permanent or longterm agreement with one company. It's simple to observe you may possibly confuse both. Afterall, both communicate the thought of performing services or work for different people or businesses.

To emphasize the gap, have a peek at the synonyms often related to each semester. Synonyms for advisers might comprise descriptors, such as for instance advisor, guru, as well as specialist. Synonyms for salespeople have a tendency to get linked with a certain career field or occupation name, & mostly a writer, journalist, writer, and graphic designer.

After selecting a freelancer, clients often consider about utilizing your services to your shortterm job with a very special outcome. As an instance, writing a example or designing a booklet. As a freelancer, then your own job is to choose initial management from the customer and then set off and finish the mission.

Typically, the job is done off-site, together with your tools and tools. You command almost every aspect of the undertaking, for example deciding on the most efficient way of handling the undertaking and deciding the essential deadline for the completion. Once the job is completed, your connection with your customer may possibly wind before another job comes together.

As a consultant, your customers turn for you for step by step assistance with a certain area of experience. By way of example, you might be hired because a catastrophe communication adviser or perhaps a marketing plan adviser providing advice to your customer. Oftentimes, the scope of the job is significantly more extensive and may comprise several smaller jobs within the total agreement.

# Don't miss out!

Visit the website below and you can sign up to receive emails whenever Daniel D. Coffman publishes a new book. There's no charge and no obligation.

https://books2read.com/r/B-A-VRLAB-DTAOC

**BOOKS 2 READ**

Connecting independent readers to independent writers.

# Also by Daniel D. Coffman

Freelance Consulting: Provide Services to High Ticket Customers. Build and Grow Your own Gig Empire.

# About the Author

Daniel D. Coffman has over 20 years of experience as a consultant with various large consulting firms and as an independent. His professional expertise spans more than 50 different industries in which he has worked as a consultant for his clients. He has seen everything from the smallest one-man operation to the largest corporation.

# About the Publisher

CREATIVITY ¦ FUN ¦ EXPERTISE

Our imprint Creafe Publishing, where creativity meets expertise, is your destination for a captivating array of books. Our extensive collection features a harmonious blend of non-fiction treasures and engaging fiction gems. We believe that learning should be an enjoyable adventure, and our commitment to 'Creativity ¦ Fun ¦ Expertise' is evident in every page we produce. Explore our catalog to discover knowledge and entertainment like never before. With Creafe Publishing, your reading journey is bound to be a delightful and enlightening experience.